아서와
사랑에 빠진 사람은
누구?

CONTENTS

대한민국 영어 학습자라면 꼭 한번 읽어봐야 할, 아서 챕터북 시리즈!

아서 챕터북 시리즈(Arthur Chapter Book series)는 미국의 작가 마크 브라운(Marc Brown)이 쓴 책입니다. 레이크우드 초등학교에 다니는 주인공 아서(Arthur)가 소소한 일상에서 벌이는 다양한 에피소드를 담은 이 책은, 기본적으로 미국 초등학생들을 위해 쓰인 책이지만 누구나 공감할 만한 재미있는 스토리로 출간된 지 30년이 넘은 지금까지 남녀노소 모두에게 큰 사랑을 받고 있습니다. 아서가 주인공으로 등장하는 이야기는 리더스북과 챕터북 등 다양한 형태로 출판되었는데, 현재 미국에서만 누적 판매 부수가 6천6백만 부를 돌파한 상황으로 대한민국 인구 숫자보다 더 많은 책이 판매된 것을 생각하면 그 인기가 어느 정도 인지 실감할 수 있습니다.

특히 이 『아서 챕터북』은 한국에서 영어 학습자를 위한 최적의 원서로 큰 사랑을 받고 있기도 합니다. 『영어 낭독 훈련』, 『잠수네 영어 학습법』, 『솔빛이네 엄마표 영어연수』 등 많은 영어 학습법 책들에서 『아서 챕터북』을 추천 도서로 선정하고 있으며, 수많은 영어 고수들과 영어 선생님들, '엄마표 영어'를 진행하는 부모님들에게도 반드시 거쳐 가야 하는 영어원서로 전폭적인 지지를 얻고 있습니다.

번역과 단어장이 포함된 워크북, 그리고 오디오북까지 담긴 풀 패키지!

이 책은 이렇게 큰 사랑을 받고 있는 영어원서 『아서 챕터북』 시리즈에, 더욱 탁월한 학습 효과를 거둘 수 있도록 다양한 콘텐츠를 덧붙인 책입니다.

- 영어원서: 본문에 나온 어려운 어휘에 볼드 처리가 되어 있어 단어를 더욱 분명히 인지하며 자연스럽게 암기하게 됩니다.
- 단어장: 원서에 나온 어려운 어휘가 '한영'은 물론 '영영' 의미까지 완벽하게 정리되어 있으며, 반복되는 단어까지 넣어두어 자연스럽게 복습이 되도록 구성했습니다.
- 번역: 영어와 비교할 수 있도록 직역에 가까운 번역을 담았습니다. 원서 읽기에 익숙하지 않는 초보 학습자들도 어려움 없이 내용을 파악할 수 있습니다.
- 퀴즈: 현직 원어민 교사가 만든 이해력 점검 퀴즈가 들어있습니다.
- 오디오북: 미국 현지에서 판매중인 빠른 속도의 오디오북(분당 약 145단어)과

국내에서 녹음된 따라 읽기용 오디오북(분당 약 110단어)을 포함하고 있어 듣기 훈련은 물론 소리 내어 읽기에까지 폭넓게 사용할 수 있습니다.

이 책의 수준과 타깃 독자
- 미국 원어민 기준: 유치원 ~ 초등학교 저학년
- 한국 학습자 기준: 초등학교 저학년 ~ 중학교 1학년
- 영어원서 완독 경험이 없는 초보 영어 학습자 (토익 기준 450~750점대)
- 비슷한 수준의 다른 챕터북: Magic Tree House, Marvin Redpost, Zack Files, Captain Underpants
- 도서 분량: 5,000단어 초반 (약 5,000~5,200단어)

아서 챕터북, 이렇게 읽어보세요!

- **단어 암기는 이렇게!** 처음 리딩을 시작하기 전, 해당 챕터에 나오는 단어들을 눈으로 쭉 훑어봅니다. 모르는 단어는 좀 더 주의 깊게 보되, 손으로 써가면서 완벽하게 암기할 필요는 없습니다. 본문을 읽으면서 이 단어들을 다시 만나게 되는데, 그 과정에서 단어의 쓰임새와 어감을 자연스럽게 익히게 됩니다. 이렇게 책을 읽은 후에, 단어를 다시 한번 복습하세요. 복습할 때는 중요하다고 생각하는 단어들을 손으로 써가면서 꼼꼼하게 외우는 것도 좋습니다. 이런 방식으로 책을 읽다보면, 많은 단어를 빠르고 부담 없이 익히게 됩니다.

- **리딩할 때는 리딩에만 집중하자!** 원서를 읽는 중간 중간 모르는 단어가 나온다고 워크북을 들춰보거나, 곧바로 번역을 찾아보는 것은 매우 좋지 않은 습관입니다. 모르는 단어나 이해가 가지 않는 문장이 나온다고 해도 펜으로 가볍게 표시만 해두고, 전체적인 맥락을 잡아가며 빠르게 읽어나가세요. 리딩을 할 때는 속도에 대한 긴장감을 잃지 않으면서 리딩에만 집중하는 것이 좋습니다. 모르는 단어와 문장은, 리딩이 끝난 후에 한꺼번에 정리해보는 '리뷰'시간을 갖습니다. 리뷰를 할 때는 번역은 물론 단어장과 사전도 꼼꼼하게 확인하면서 왜 이해가 되지 않았는지 확인해 봅니다.

- **번역 활용은 이렇게!** 이해가 가지 않는 문장은 번역을 통해서 그 의미를 파악할

수 있습니다. 하지만 한국어와 영어는 정확히 1:1 대응이 되지 않기 때문에 번역을 활용하는 데에도 지혜가 필요합니다. 의역이 된 부분까지 억지로 의미를 대응해서 암기하려고 하기보다, 어떻게 그런 의미가 만들어진 것인지 추측하면서 번역은 참고자료로 활용하는 것이 좋습니다.

- **듣기 훈련은 이렇게!** 리스닝 실력을 향상시키길 원한다면 오디오북을 적극적으로 활용하세요. 처음에는 오디오북을 틀어놓고 눈으로 해당 내용을 따라 읽으면서 훈련을 하고, 이것이 익숙해지면 오디오북만 틀어놓고 '귀를 통해' 책을 읽어보세요. 눈으로는 한 번도 읽지 않은 책을 귀를 통해 완벽하게 이해할 수 있다면 이후에는 영어 듣기로 고생하는 일은 거의 없을 것입니다.

- **소리 내어 읽고 녹음하자!** 이 책은 특히 소리 내어 읽기(Voice Reading)에 최적화된 문장 길이와 구조를 가지고 있습니다. 또한 오디오북 CD에 포함된 '따라 읽기용' 오디오북으로 소리 내어 읽기 훈련을 함께할 수 있습니다. 소리 내어 읽기를 하면서 내가 읽은 것을 녹음하고 들어보세요! 자신의 영어 발음을 들어보는 것은 몹시 민망한 일이지만, 그 과정을 통해서 의식적 · 무의식적으로 발음을 교정하게 됩니다. 이렇게 영어로 소리를 만들어 본 경험은 이후 탄탄한 스피킹 실력의 밑거름이 될 것입니다.

- **2~3번 반복해서 읽자!** 영어 초보자라면 2~3회 반복해서 읽을 것을 추천합니다. 초보자일수록 처음 읽을 때는 생소한 단어들과 스토리 때문에 내용 파악에 급급할 수밖에 없습니다. 하지만 일단 내용을 파악한 후에 다시 읽으면 어휘와 문장 구조 등 다른 부분까지 관찰하면서 조금 더 깊이 있게 읽을 수 있고, 그 과정에서 리딩 속도도 빨라지고 리딩 실력을 더 확고하게 다지게 됩니다.

- **'시리즈'로 꾸준히 읽자!** 한 작가의 책을 시리즈로 읽는 것 또한 영어 실력 향상에 큰 도움이 됩니다. 같은 등장인물이 다시 나오기 때문에 내용 파악이 더 수월할 뿐 아니라, 작가가 사용하는 어휘와 표현들도 자연스럽게 반복되기 때문에 탁월한 복습 효과까지 얻을 수 있습니다. 『아서 챕터북』 시리즈는 현재 10권, 총 50,000단어 분량이 출간되어 있습니다. 이 책들을 시리즈로 꾸준히 읽으면서 영어 실력을 쑥쑥 향상시켜 보세요!

영어원서 본문 구성

After Mr. Ratburn dismissed them, Francine, Muffy, and Arthur headed for the school yard.

"You're doing it again," said Francine.

"Doing what?" asked Muffy.

"Mumbling," Francine folded her arms. "Come on, what's the matter?"

Muffy folded her arms, too. "Well, if you must know, I was just saying what a crummy day this was."

Arthur nodded. "I don't like the rain, either."

"No, not that," said Muffy. "I'm talking about the dancing."

"Oh, that," said Francine, laughing. "You did have your hands full. But I think Binky's getting better."

Muffy snorted. "Maybe so, but I don't know if I'll survive another hoedown like that." She suddenly brightened. "Hey, Arthur! Next time we have square dancing, will you be my partner?"

Arthur shrugged. "Okay," he said.

9

내용이 담긴 본문입니다.
원어민이 읽는 일반 원서와 같은 텍스트지만, 암기해야 할 중요 어휘들은 볼드체로 표시되어 있습니다. 이 어휘들은 지금 들고 계신 워크북에 챕터별로 정리되어 있습니다.

학습 심리학 연구 결과에 따르면, 한 단어씩 따로 외우는 단어 암기는 거의 효과가 없다고 합니다. 대신 단어를 제대로 외우기 위해서는 문맥(Context) 속에서 단어를 암기해야 하며, 한 단어 당 문맥 속에서 15번 이상 마주칠 때 완벽하게 암기할 수 있다고 합니다.

이 책의 본문은 중요 어휘를 볼드로 강조하여, 문맥 속의 단어들을 더 확실히 인지(Word Cognition in Context)하도록 돕고 있습니다. 또한 대부분의 중요한 단어들은 다른 챕터에서도 반복해서 등장하기 때문에 이 책을 읽는 것만으로도 자연스럽게 어휘력을 향상시킬 수 있습니다.

또한 본문에는 내용 이해를 돕기 위해 '각주'가 첨가되어 있습니다. 각주는 굳이 암기할 필요는 없지만, 알아두면 내용을 더 깊이 있게 이해할 수 있어 원서를 읽는 재미가 배가됩니다.

Arms swinging madly, Binky hoedowned* backward to his spot. His elbow knocked the Brain to one side. The Brain stepped on Sue Ellen's foot. Sue Ellen slipped and fell onto Francine. In another moment, they were all slipping, falling, and most of all, complaining.

Mrs. MacGrady shut off the boom box. "I think that's enough for today," she said. "You were all very light on your feet." She glanced at Binky. "And I know the rest of you are trying your best."

Gym was the last class of the day. All the kids returned to Mr. Ratburn's classroom to gather their things before the bell rang.

"Did you say something?" Francine asked Muffy as she passed Muffy's desk.

"No," said Muffy.

* hoedown(n) 흥겨운 그룹댄스를 '하다'라는 의미로서, 여기서는 춤사로 추며 '발을 헛디뎌 균형을 잃으면서 뒤로' 넘어지는 것을 표현

* boom box 대형 라디오 카세트 플레이어

8

워크북(Workbook)의 구성

Check Your Reading Speed

해당 챕터의 단어 수가 기록되어 있어, 리딩 속도를 측정할 수 있습니다. 특히 리딩 속도를 중시하는 독자들이 유용하게 사용할 수 있습니다.

Build Your Vocabulary

본문에 볼드 표시되어 있는 단어들이 정리되어 있습니다. 리딩 전, 후에 반복해서 보면 원서를 더욱 쉽게 읽을 수 있고, 어휘력도 빠르게 향상됩니다.

단어는 〈빈도 – 스펠링 – 발음기호 – 품사 – 한글 뜻 – 영문 뜻〉 순서로 표기되어 있으며 빈도 표시(★)가 많을수록 필수 어휘입니다. 반복 등장하는 단어는 빈도 대신 '복습'으로 표기되어 있습니다. 품사는 아래와 같이 표기했습니다.

n. 명사 ｜ a. 형용사 ｜ ad. 부사 ｜ v. 동사

conj. 접속사 ｜ prep. 전치사 ｜ int. 감탄사 ｜ idiom 숙어 및 관용구

Comprehension Quiz

간단한 퀴즈를 통해 읽은 내용에 대한 이해력을 점검해 볼 수 있습니다.

번역

영문과 비교할 수 있도록 최대한 직역에 가까운 번역을 담았습니다.

오디오북 CD 구성

이 책은 '듣기 훈련'과 '소리 내어 읽기 훈련'을
위한 2가지 종류의 오디오북이 포함되어 있습
니다.

- 듣기 훈련용 오디오북: 분당 145단어 속도
  (미국 현지 판매 중인 오디오북)
- 소리 내어 읽기 훈련용 오디오북: 분당 110
  단어 속도
오디오북은 MP3 파일로 제공되는 MP3 기기나
컴퓨터에 옮겨서 사용하셔야 합니다. 오디오북
에 이상이 있을 경우 helper@longtailbooks.co.kr로 메일을 주시면 자세한 안내를
받으실 수 있습니다.

EBS 동영상 강의 안내

EBS의 어학사이트(EBSlang.co.kr)에서 『아서 챕터북』동영상 강의가 진행되고 있습니다.
영어 어순의 원리에 맞게 빠르고 정확하게 이해하는 법을 완벽하게 코치해주는 국내 유일의 강의!
저렴한 수강료에 완강 시 50% 환급까지!
지금 바로 열광적인 수강 평가와 샘플 강의를 확인하세요!
http://EBSreading.com

Chapter 1

1. **When did the students at Lakewood Elementary school do square dancing?**
   A. On Fridays
   B. On test days
   C. On rainy days
   D. On weekends

2. **How did Binky dance?**
   A. He bumped into people.
   B. He was light on his feet.
   C. He danced like an expert.
   D. He danced like a helicopter.

3. Why was Muffy complaining about the day?

A. She was feeling sick.

B. She didn't like the rain.

C. She had to dance with Binky.

D. She didn't want to do homework.

4. What did Muffy ask Arthur to do?

A. She asked him to tie Binky's shoelaces.

B. She asked him to be her dance partner.

C. She asked him to help Binky improve.

D. She asked him to dance with Binky instead.

5. How did Francine react when Muffy started to argue?

A. She told Arthur to stop listening to Muffy.

B. She dragged Arthur away to give him a ride home.

C. She told Muffy that she didn't have a say in it.

D. She told Muffy that she could dance with Arthur later.

1분에 몇 단어를 읽는지 리딩 속도를 측정해보세요.

$$\frac{568 \ words}{reading \ time \ (\quad) \ sec} \times 60 = (\quad) \ WPM$$

Build Your Vocabulary

‡ **gym** [dʒim] n. (= gymnasium) 체육관; (특히 학교에서 하는) 운동
A gym is a club, building, or large room, usually containing special equipment, where people go to do physical exercise and get fit.

‡ **tradition** [trədíʃən] n. 전통
A tradition is a custom or belief that has existed for a long time.

* **cafeteria** [kæfətíəriə] n. 구내식당 (school cafeteria n. 교내 식당)
A cafeteria is a restaurant where you choose your food from a counter and take it to your table after paying for it.

‡ **lead** [liːd] ① v. (led–led) 이끌다; 지휘하다; 선두를 달리다; n. 선두, 우세 ② n. [광물] 납
If you lead a group of people, an organization, or an activity, you are in control or in charge of the people or the activity.

‡ **swing** [swiŋ] v. (swung–swung) 휙 돌리다; 흔들다; 휘두르다; n. 흔들기; 휘두르기
If something swings or if you swing it, it moves repeatedly backward and forward or from side to side from a fixed point.

‡ **complain** [kəmpléin] v. 불평하다, 투덜거리다
If you complain about a situation, you say that you are not satisfied with it.

* **clap** [klæp] v. 손뼉을 치다; 박수를 치다; n. 박수, 손뼉
When you clap, you hit your hands together to show appreciation or attract attention.

high five [hài fáiv] v. 하이파이브를 하다; n. 하이파이브
If you high five with someone, you greet them by slapping the palms of their raised arms with your own.

scoot [sku:t] v. 빨리 가다; 돌진하다, 뛰어나가다
If you scoot somewhere, you go there very quickly.

lumber [lʌ́mbər] v. 느릿느릿 움직이다; (방 등을) 어지르다; n. 잡동사니; 재목
If someone or something lumbers from one place to another, they move there very slowly and clumsily.

forward [fɔ́:rwərd] ad. 앞으로; 미래로; 더 일찍, 빨리; a. 앞으로 가는; v. (물건·정보를) 보내다
If you move or look forward, you move or look in a direction that is in front of you.

yank [jæŋk] v. 홱 잡아당기다; n. 홱 잡아당기기
If you yank someone or something somewhere, you pull them there suddenly and with a lot of force.

look out idiom 주의해라, 조심해라
When you say 'look out' to someone, you tell them to be careful, especially when there is some danger.

hurl [hə:rl] v. (거칠게) 던지다; 욕, 비난 등을 퍼붓다
If you hurl something, you throw it violently and with a lot of force.

balance [bǽləns] n. 균형, 평형; v. 균형을 유지하다; 균형을 이루다
(off-balance a. 균형을 잃은)
If someone or something is off-balance, they can easily fall or be knocked over because they are not standing firmly.

watch it idiom (경고의 의미로) 조심해
You say 'watch it' in order to warn someone to be careful, especially when you want to threaten them.

pick oneself up idiom (넘어졌다가) 일어서다
If you pick yourself up, you stand up again after a fall.

fault [fɔːlt] n. 잘못, 책임; 단점; 결함; v. 나무라다, 흠잡다
If a bad or undesirable situation is your fault, you caused it or are responsible for it.

backward [bǽkwərd] ad. 뒤로; 거꾸로, 반대 방향으로; a. 뒤의; 뒷걸음질하는, 퇴보하는
If you move or look backward, you move or look in the direction that your back is facing.

spot [spat] n. 곳, 장소; (작은) 점; 얼룩; v. 발견하다, 찾다, 알아채다
You can refer to a particular place as a spot.

elbow [élbou] n. 팔꿈치; v. (팔꿈치로) 밀치다
Your elbow is the part of your arm where the upper and lower halves of the arm are joined.

knock [nak] v. 치다; 부딪치다; (문을) 두드리다; n. 문 두드리는 소리; 부딪침
To knock someone into a particular position or condition means to hit them very hard so that they fall over or become unconscious.

step on idiom ~을 (짓)밟다; ~을 해치다
If you step on something or step in a particular direction, you put your foot on the thing or move your foot in that direction.

slip [slip] v. 미끄러지다; 빠져 나가다; 슬며시 가다; n. (작은) 실수; 미끄러짐
If you slip, you accidentally slide and lose your balance.

light on one's feet idiom 동작이 빠르다
If someone is light on their feet, they can move quickly and are agile.

glance [glæns] v. 흘낏 보다; 대충 훑어보다; n. 흘낏 봄
If you glance at something or someone, you look at them very quickly and then look away again immediately.

rest [rest] n. 나머지 (사람들·것들); 휴식; v. 쉬다; 기대다
The rest is used to refer to all the parts of something or all the things in a group that remain or that you have not already mentioned.

gather [gǽðər] v. (여기저기 있는 것을) 모으다; (사람들이) 모이다
If you gather things, you collect them together so that you can use them.

dismiss [dismís] v. (사람을) 물러가게 하다; 묵살하다, 일축하다
If you are dismissed by someone in authority, they tell you that you can go away from them.

head [hed] v. (특정 방향으로) 향하다; ~을 이끌다, 책임지다; n. 머리, 고개; 책임자
If you are heading for a particular place, you are going toward that place.

yard [jaːrd] n. 마당, 뜰 (school yard n. 학교 운동장)
The school yard is the large open area with a hard surface just outside a school building, where the schoolchildren can play and do other activities.

mumble [mʌmbl] v. 중얼거리다, 웅얼거리다; n. 중얼거림
If you mumble, you speak very quietly and not at all clearly with the result that the words are difficult to understand.

fold [fould] v. (두 손·팔 등을) 끼다; 접다; 감싸다; n. 주름; 접는 부분
If you fold your arms or hands, you bring them together and cross or link them, for example over your chest.

come on idiom 자 어서, 서둘러
You use 'come on' to encourage someone do something, for example, to hurry.

matter [mǽtər] n. 문제, 일; 물질; 상황; v. 중요하다; 문제되다
You use matter in expressions such as 'What's the matter?' or 'Is anything the matter?' when you think that someone has a problem and you want to know what it is.

crummy [krʌ́mi] a. 형편없는, 초라한
Something that is crummy is unpleasant, of very poor quality, or not good enough.

nod [nad] v. (고개를) 끄덕이다, 끄덕여 나타내다; n. (고개를) 끄덕임
If you nod, you move your head downward and upward to show agreement, understanding, or approval.

have one's hands full idiom 아주 바쁘다, (다른 일을 할) 짬이 안 나다
If you have your hands full with something, you are very busy because of it.

snort [snɔːrt] v. 코웃음을 치다, 콧방귀를 뀌다; n. 코웃음, 콧방귀
If someone snorts something, they say it in a way that shows contempt.

survive [sərváiv] v. 견뎌 내다; 살아남다, 생존하다
If you survive in difficult circumstances, you manage to live or continue in spite of them and do not let them affect you very much.

brighten [braitn] v. (얼굴 등이) 환해지다; 밝아지다
If someone brightens or their face brightens, they suddenly look happier.

shrug [ʃrʌg] v. (어깨를) 으쓱하다; n. (어깨를) 으쓱하기
If you shrug, you raise your shoulders to show that you are not interested in something or that you do not know or care about something.

frown [fraun] v. 얼굴을 찌푸리다; n. 찡그림, 찌푸림
When someone frowns, their eyebrows become drawn together, because they are annoyed or puzzled.

burst [bəːrst] v. (burst-burst) 불쑥 움직이다; 터지다, 파열하다; n. (갑자기) 한바탕 ~을 함; 파열
To burst into or out of a place means to enter or leave it suddenly with a lot of energy or force.

shoelace [ʃúːleis] n. 신발끈
Shoelaces are long, narrow pieces of material like pieces of string that you use to fasten your shoes.

tie [tai] v. (끈 등으로) 묶다; 결부시키다; n. 끈; (강한) 유대관계 (untied a. 묶이지 않은)
When you untie your shoelaces or your shoes, you loosen or undo the laces of your shoes.

trip [trip] v. 발을 헛디디다; ~를 넘어뜨리다; n. 여행; 발을 헛디딤
If you trip when you are walking, you knock your foot against something and fall or nearly fall.

tumble [tʌmbl] v. 굴러 떨어지다; 폭삭 무너지다; n. 굴러 떨어짐; 폭락
If someone or something tumbles somewhere, they fall there with a rolling or bouncing movement.

bounce [bauns] v. 튀(기)다; 흔들거리며 가다; n. 튐, 튀어 오름
When an object such as a ball bounces or when you bounce it, it moves upward from a surface or away from it immediately after hitting it.

on purpose idiom 고의로, 일부러
If you do something on purpose, you do it intentionally.

wonder [wʌ́ndər] v. 궁금해하다; (크게) 놀라다; n. 경탄, 경이
If you wonder about something, you think about it because it interests you and you want to know more about it.

insurance [inʃúərəns] n. 보험; (미래의 불행에 대비한) 보호 수단
Insurance is an arrangement in which you pay money to a company, and they pay money to you if something unpleasant happens to you.

stick with idiom ~의 곁에 머물다; ~을 계속하다
If you stick with someone, you continue using them to do work for you, and not stop or change to someone else.

get a say idiom 발언권이 있다; 참견할 권리가 있다
If you get a say in something, you have the right to give your opinion and influence decisions relating to it.

argue [áːrgjuː] v. 언쟁을 하다; 주장하다
If one person argues with another, they speak angrily to each other about something that they disagree about.

cut in idiom (말·대화에) 끼어들다, (남의 말을) 자르다
To cut in means to interrupt someone who is speaking.

lift [lift] n. (차 등을) 태워 주기; (들어)올리기; v. 들어 올리다, 올리다
If you give someone a lift somewhere, you take them there in your car as a favor to them.

* **drag** [dræg] v. 끌다; 힘들게 움직이다; (원치 않는 곳에) 가게 하다; n. 끌기; 장애물
If someone drags you somewhere, they pull you there, or force you to
go there by physically threatening you.

* **garbage** [gáːrbidʒ] n. 쓰레기, 찌꺼기 (garbage truck n. 쓰레기 수거차)
A garbage truck is a large truck which collects the garbage from outside
people's houses.

: **expression** [ikspréʃən] n. 표정; 표현, 표출
Your expression is the way that your face looks at a particular moment.
It shows what you are thinking or feeling.

Chapter 2

1. What was Muffy's mood like when the rain had stopped?

   A. Her mood was lighthearted.

   B. Her mood was still dark.

   C. Her mood was brighter.

   D. Her mood was still silly.

2. How did Binky first react to Muffy saying that her dance partner was always stepping on her toes?

   A. He said that was only natural.

   B. He said that was not very considerate.

   C. He said that she should find a different partner.

   D. He said that he had a partner who did the same thing.

3. How did Binky feel about the other students swinging their partners while dancing?

   A. He felt that their partners weren't strong enough.

   B. He felt that they didn't know their own strength.

   C. He felt that they didn't understand the dance.

   D. He felt that they couldn't feel pain.

4. Why was Muffy mad at Francine?

   A. Francine had stepped on Muffy's toes.

   B. Francine had said mean things about her to Binky.

   C. Francine was a great dancer.

   D. Francine wouldn't share Arthur with her.

5. Why did Binky think that Francine did not want to share Arthur?

   A. Binky thought that Francine couldn't dance well without Arthur.

   B. Binky thought that Francine wanted to speak her mind with Arthur.

   C. Binky thought that Francine and Arthur must be in love.

   D. Binky thought that Francine was Arthur's best friend.

Check Your Reading Speed
1분에 몇 단어를 읽는지 리딩 속도를 측정해보세요.

$$\frac{464 \ words}{reading \ time \ (\qquad) \ sec} \times 60 = (\qquad) \ WPM$$

Build Your Vocabulary

* **sigh** [sai] v. 한숨을 쉬다, 한숨짓다; n. 한숨; 탄식
When you sigh, you let out a deep breath, as a way of expressing feelings such as disappointment, tiredness, or pleasure.

peek [pi:k] v. 살짝 보이다; (재빨리) 훔쳐보다; n. 엿보기
If something is peeking out from somewhere, they are sticking out slightly so as to be just visible.

✲ **mood** [mu:d] n. 기분; 분위기
Your mood is the way you are feeling at a particular time.

복습 **tie** [tai] v. (끈 등으로) 묶다; 결부시키다; n. 끈; (강한) 유대관계 (retie v. ~을 새로 묶다)
If you tie two things together or tie them, you fasten them together with a knot.

sneaker [sníːkər] n. (pl.) 운동화
Sneakers are casual shoes with rubber soles.

✲ **knot** [nat] n. 매듭; (복부·목 등이) 뻣뻣한 느낌; v. 매듭을 묶다
If you tie a knot in a piece of string, rope, cloth, or other material, you pass one end or part of it through a loop and pull it tight.

envelop [invéləp] v. 감싸다, 뒤덮다
If one thing envelops another, it covers or surrounds it completely.

cocoon [kəkúːn] n. 보호막; (곤충의) 고치; v. ~을 보호하다
If you are in a cocoon of something, you are wrapped up in it or surrounded by it.

comfort [kΛmfərt] n. 안락, 편안; 위로, 위안; v. 위로하다
If you are doing something in comfort, you are physically relaxed and contented, and are not feeling any pain or other unpleasant sensations.

step on idiom ~을 (짓)밟다; ~을 해치다
If you step on something or step in a particular direction, you put your foot on the thing or move your foot in that direction.

toe [tou] n. 발가락
Your toes are the five movable parts at the end of each foot.

nod [nad] v. (고개를) 끄덕이다, 끄덕여 나타내다; n. (고개를) 끄덕임
If you nod, you move your head downward and upward to show agreement, understanding, or approval.

considerate [kənsídərət] a. 사려 깊은, (남을) 배려하는
Someone who is considerate pays attention to the needs, wishes, or feelings of other people.

confuse [kənfjúːz] v. (사람을) 혼란시키다; 혼동하다 (confused a. 혼란스러워 하는)
If you are confused, you do not know exactly what is happening or what to do.

scratch [skrætʃ] v. 긁다, 할퀴다; 긁히는 소리를 내다; n. 긁힌 자국; 긁히는 소리
If you scratch yourself, you rub your fingernails against your skin because it is itching.

strength [streŋkθ] n. 힘, 기운; 내구력, 견고성
Your strength is the physical energy that you have, which gives you the ability to perform various actions, such as lifting or moving things.

swing [swiŋ] v. 휙 돌리다; 흔들다; 휘두르다; n. 흔들기; 휘두르기
If something swings or if you swing it, it moves repeatedly backward and forward or from side to side from a fixed point.

notice [nóutis] v. ~을 의식하다, (보거나 듣고) 알다; 주목하다; n. 주목; 안내문
If you notice something or someone, you become aware of them.

figure [fígjər] v. 생각하다, 판단하다; 중요하다; n. 수치; (멀리서 흐릿하게 보이는) 모습
If you figure that something is the case, you think or guess that it is the case.

pace [peis] v. 서성거리다; (일의) 속도를 유지하다; n. 속도; 걸음
If you pace a small area, you keep walking up and down it, because you are anxious or impatient.

fault [fɔːlt] n. 잘못, 책임; 단점; 결함; v. 나무라다, 흠잡다
If a bad or undesirable situation is your fault, you caused it or are responsible for it.

knowing [nóuiŋ] a. (비밀로 되어 있는 일을) 다 안다는 듯한
(knowingly ad. 다 알고 있다는 듯이; (사정 등을) 다 알고도, 고의로)
If you knowingly do something, you do that in a way that suggests you have secret knowledge or awareness.

personal [pə́rsənl] a. 개인의, 개인적인; 직접 한
A personal opinion, quality, or thing belongs or relates to one particular person rather than to other people.

property [prápərti] n. 재산, 소유물; 소유지
Someone's property is all the things that belong to them or something that belongs to them.

horrify [hɔ́ːrəfài] v. 몸서리치게 하다, 소름 끼치게 하다 (horrified a. 충격 받은)
If someone is horrified, they feel shocked or disgusted, because of something that they have seen or heard.

no way idiom 말도 안돼; 절대로 안 돼, 싫어
You can say no way as an emphatic way of saying no.

roll one's eyes idiom 눈을 굴리다
If you roll your eyes, you move them round and upward when you are frightened, bored, or annoyed.

afraid [əfréid] a. 두려워하는, 겁내는; 걱정하는
If you are afraid of someone or afraid to do something, you are frightened because you think that something very unpleasant is going to happen to you.

keep one's hands off idiom ~에 간섭하지 않다; ~을 손대지 않다
If you tell someone to keep their hands off something, you are telling them in a rather aggressive way not to touch it or interfere with it.

speak one's mind idiom 생각을 털어놓다, 생각한 대로 서슴없이 말하다
If you speak your mind, you say firmly and honestly what you think about a situation, even if this may offend or upset people.

wonder [wÁndər] v. 궁금해하다; (크게) 놀라다; n. 경탄, 경이
If you wonder about something, you think about it because it interests you and you want to know more about it.

sideways [sáidwèiz] ad. 옆으로; 옆에서
Sideways means from or towards the side of something or someone.

glance [glæns] v. 흘낏 보다; 대충 훑어보다; n. 흘낏 봄
If you glance at something or someone, you look at them very quickly and then look away again immediately.

ride [raid] v. (rode-ridden) (자전거·오토바이·말 등을) 타다; n. (차량·자전거 등을) 타고 달리기; 여정
When you ride a bicycle or a motorcycle, you sit on it, control it, and travel along on it.

arm in arm idiom 서로 팔짱을 끼고
If two people are walking arm in arm, they are walking together with their arms linked.

shudder [ʃÁdər] v. (공포·추위 등으로) 몸을 떨다, 몸서리치다; n. 몸이 떨림, 전율
If you shudder, you shake with fear, horror, or disgust, or because you are cold.

Chapter 3

1. What was Arthur still thinking about from the day before?

A. He was thinking about what was going on between Muffy and Francine.

B. He was thinking about dancing with Muffy instead of Francine.

C. He was thinking about how well he danced with Francine.

D. He was thinking about what Muffy and Binky had discussed.

2. What did Binky ask Arthur at the bike rack?

A. He asked if he could copy his homework.

B. He asked if he could borrow his bike.

C. He asked about Arthur's girlfriend.

D. He asked about Arthur's dancing.

3. How did Arthur feel about the idea of Francine being his girlfriend?
   A. He thought it was scary.
   B. He thought it was funny.
   C. He thought it was nice.
   D. He thought it was a good idea.

4. What surprise did Francine have for Arthur?
   A. She got two pairs of cowboy boots.
   B. She got two cowboy pants.
   C. She got two cowboy shirts.
   D. She got two cowboy hats.

5. Why did Francine decide to surprise Arthur?
   A. She was in love with Arthur.
   B. She thought they could wear them at the next square dance.
   C. It was Arthur's birthday and she wanted to give him a present.
   D. Arthur had surprised her a week before and she wanted to return the favor.

Check Your Reading Speed

1분에 몇 단어를 읽는지 리딩 속도를 측정해보세요.

$$\frac{528 \ words}{reading\ time\ (\quad)\ sec} \times 60 = (\qquad)\ WPM$$

Build Your Vocabulary

_{복습} ride [raid] v. (rode–ridden) (자전거·오토바이·말 등을) 타다;
n. (차량·자전거 등을) 타고 달리기; 여정
When you ride a bicycle or a motorcycle, you sit on it, control it, and travel along on it.

_{복습} certain [səːrtn] a. 확실한, 틀림없는; 확신하는
If you say that something is certain, you firmly believe that it is true, or have definite knowledge about it.

figure out idiom ~을 이해하다, 알아내다
If you figure someone or something out, you finally understand them, or find the solution to a problem after a lot of thought.

rack [ræk] n. 받침대; 선반; v. 괴롭히다, 고통을 주다 (**bike rack** n. 자전거 고정대)
A rack is a frame or shelf, usually with bars or hooks, that is used for holding things or for hanging things on.

_{복습} fold [fould] v. (두 손·팔 등을) 끼다; 접다; 감싸다; n. 주름; 접는 부분
If you fold your arms or hands, you bring them together and cross or link them, for example over your chest.

hint [hint] n. 힌트, 암시; 기미, 흔적; v. 넌지시 알려주다
A hint is a suggestion about something that is made in an indirect way.

initial [iníʃəl] n. (이름·명칭의) 머리글자, 첫 글자; a. 처음의, 초기의
Initials are the capital letters which begin each word of a name.

blink [bliŋk] v. 눈을 깜박이다; (불빛이) 깜박거리다; n. 눈을 깜박거림
When you blink or when you blink your eyes, you shut your eyes and very quickly open them again.

hip [hip] n. 허리; 둔부, 엉덩이
Your hips are the two areas at the sides of your body between the tops of your legs and your waist.

ridiculous [ridíkjuləs] a. 말도 안 되는, 터무니없는, 웃기는
If you say that something or someone is ridiculous, you mean that they are very foolish.

wink [wiŋk] v. 윙크하다; (빛이) 깜박거리다; n. 윙크
When you wink at someone, you look toward them and close one eye very briefly, usually as a signal that something is a joke or a secret.

argue [á:rgju:] v. 언쟁을 하다; 주장하다
If one person argues with another, they speak angrily to each other about something that they disagree about.

bellow [bélou] v. (우렁찬 소리로) 고함치다; 크게 울리다; n. 울부짖는 소리; 고함소리
If someone bellows, they shout angrily in a loud, deep voice.

locker [lákər] n. (자물쇠가 달린) 사물함
A locker is a small metal or wooden cupboard with a lock, where you can put your personal possessions.

absurd [æbsə́:rd] a. 우스꽝스러운, 터무니없는
If you say that something is absurd, you are criticizing it because you think that it is ridiculous or that it does not make sense.

silly [síli] a. 어리석은, 바보 같은; 유치한; n. 바보
If you say that someone or something is silly, you mean that they are foolish, childish, or ridiculous.

goofy [gú:fi] a. 바보 같은, 얼빠진
If you describe someone or something as goofy, you think they are rather silly or ridiculous.

in fact idiom 사실은, 실은; 실제로는
You use in fact to indicate that you are giving more detailed information about what you have just said.

reach [riːʃ] v. (손·팔을) 뻗다, 내밀다; 이르다, 도달하다; n. 거리; 범위
If you reach somewhere, you move your arm and hand to take or touch something.

hold on idiom 기다려, 멈춰; 견뎌 내다
If you ask someone to hold on, you are asking them to wait or stop for a short time.

fish out idiom ~을 꺼내다, ~을 빼내다
If you fish out something, you take or pull them out of a bag or other container.

basement [béismənt] n. (건물의) 지하층
The basement of a building is a floor built partly or completely below ground level.

range [reindʒ] n. 방목장; 다양성; 범위; v. 다양하다; 포함하다
A range is a large area of land on a farm where cows or other animals are kept.

round up idiom (소·양 등을) 모아 들이다; ~을 (찾아) 모으다
To round up means to bring together a number of people, animals or objects in one place.

dogie [dóugi] n. 어미 잃은 송아지
A dogie is a motherless calf.

doggie [dɔ́ːgi] n. (= doggy) (아이들 말로) 개; a. 개의, 개와 같은
Doggie is a child's word for a dog.

cattle [kætl] n. 소
Cattle are cows and bulls.

plunk [plʌŋk] v. 탁 하고 내려놓다; 털썩 앉다; n. 쿵 (하는 소리)
If you plunk something somewhere, you put it or drop it there heavily and carelessly.

care [kɛər] v. 좋아하다, 하고 싶어하다; 상관하다, 관심을 가지다; 배려하다;
n. 보살핌; 주의
You can ask someone if they would care for something or if they would care to do something as a polite way of asking if they would like to have or do something.

pardner [páːrdnər] n. (격식을 갖추지 않는 호칭으로) 파트너
Pardner refers to a friend or partner and it is used as a term of address.

tug [tʌg] v. (세게) 잡아당기다; 끌어당기다; n. 잡아당김
If you tug something or tug at it, you give it a quick and usually strong pull.

brim [brim] n. (모자의) 챙; v. (넘칠 듯) 그득하다; 가득 채우다
The brim of a hat is the wide part that sticks outward at the bottom.

proud [praud] a. 자랑스러워하는; 자존심이 강한; 오만한, 거만한
If you feel proud, you feel pleased about something good that you possess or have done, or about something good that a person close to you has done.

twirl [twəːrl] n. 빙그르르 돌기; v. 빙글빙글 돌다; 빙빙 돌리다, 회전시키다
Twirl refers to the act of rotating rapidly.

spin [spin] v. (spun-spun) (휙) 돌아서다; 돌리다, 회전시키다; n. 회전, 돌기
If something spins or if you spin it, it turns quickly around a central point.

hall [hɔːl] n. (건물 안의) 복도; 현관; 넓은 방, 홀
A hall in a building is a long passage with doors into rooms on both sides of it.

whisper [hwíspər] v. 속삭이다, 소곤거리다; n. 속삭임, 소곤거리는 소리
When you whisper, you say something very quietly.

warn [wɔːrn] v. 경고하다, 주의를 주다; 강력히 충고하다 (warning n. 경고, 주의)

A warning is something which is said or written to tell people of a possible danger, problem, or other unpleasant thing that might happen.

dizzy [dízi] a. 어지러운; 아찔한

If you feel dizzy, you feel that you are losing your balance and are about to fall.

by the way idiom 그런데

You say 'by the way' when you add something to what you are saying, especially something that you have just thought of.

Chapter 4

1. **What activity was the class doing in the afternoon?**

   A. Chess

   B. Basketball

   C. Baseball

   D. Square dance

2. **Why was Francine not using her old glove?**

   A. She had a new glove to break in.

   B. She had accidentally thrown it away.

   C. She wanted to play without a glove.

   D. It wasn't clean enough to use.

3. How did Muffy feel about Francine's glove?

   A. She thought it was very nice.

   B. She thought it was very expensive.

   C. She thought it was used and didn't fit her.

   D. She thought that Francine should throw it away.

4. Why was Francine's glove so special?

   A. Her father had given it to her.

   B. She had won it at school.

   C. She had her name written on it.

   D. She had won the championship with it.

5. What swept away Binky's doubts about Arthur and Francine?

   A. Francine giving Arthur her glove

   B. Francine giving Arthur a cowboy hat

   C. Francine playing baseball with Arthur

   D. Francine smiling and waving at Arthur

$$\frac{532 \ words}{reading \ time \ (\qquad) \ sec} \times 60 = (\qquad) \ WPM$$

Build Your Vocabulary

locker [lákər] n. (자물쇠가 달린) 사물함 (locker room n. (학교·체육관 등의) 탈의실)
A locker room is a room with lockers where people can keep clothes and other things, especially while taking part in a sport.

field [fiːld] n. 경기장, 구장; 들, 들판; (도서관·실험실 등이 아닌) 현장
A sports field is an area of grass where sports are played.

glove [glʌv] n. 야구 글러브; 장갑
A baseball glove is a large glove worn by a player whose job involves catching the ball.

break in idiom (새 물건을) 길을 들이다; ~을 훈련시키다
To break in something means to wear new shoes or use new equipment for short periods to make them more comfortable.

amazing [əméiziŋ] a. (감탄스럽도록) 놀라운, 멋진
You say that something is amazing when it is very surprising and makes you feel pleasure, approval, or wonder.

snag [snæg] v. 잡아채다, 낚아채다; 걸리다, 찢기다; n. 날카로운 것
If you snag something, you get or catch it by acting quickly.

magnet [mǽgnit] n. 자석; 매료하는 사람
A magnet is a piece of iron or other material which attracts iron toward it.

inspect [inspékt] v. 점검하다, 검사하다; 사찰하다
If you inspect something, you look at every part of it carefully in order to find out about it or check that it is all right.

fit [fit] v. (모양·크기가) 맞다; 적절하다; a. 어울리는, 적합한
If something fits, it is the right size and shape to go onto a person's body or onto a particular object.

proper [prápər] a. 적절한, 제대로 된; 올바른, 정당한 (properly ad. 제대로, 적절히)
If something is done properly, it is done in a correct and satisfactory way.

shrug [ʃrʌg] v. (어깨를) 으쓱하다; n. (어깨를) 으쓱하기
If you shrug, you raise your shoulders to show that you are not interested in something or that you do not know or care about something.

sneaker [sníːkər] n. (pl.) 운동화
Sneakers are casual shoes with rubber soles.

weigh [wei] v. 무게를 달다; 따져 보다, 저울질하다
If you weigh something or someone, you measure how heavy they are.

cut it out idiom 그만둬
You can use 'cut it out' for telling someone to stop doing something that you do not like.

besides [bisáidz] ad. 게다가, 뿐만 아니라; prep. 외에
Besides is used to emphasize an additional point that you are making, especially one that you consider to be important.

smack [smæk] v. 크게 소리를 내며 키스하다; 세게 부딪치다; n. 때리기; 탁 (하는 소리)
If you are smacking, you are kissing noisily.

argue [áːrgjuː] v. 언쟁을 하다; 주장하다
If one person argues with another, they speak angrily to each other about something that they disagree about.

triumphant [traiʌ́mfənt] a. 의기양양한; 크게 성공한 (triumphantly ad. 의기양양하여)
Someone who is triumphant has gained a victory or succeeded in something and feels very happy about it.

public [pʌ́blik] n. 일반 사람들, 대중; a. 일반인의, 대중의; 대중을 위한, 공공의
If you say or do something in public, you say or do it when a group of people are present.

headache [hédeik] n. 두통; 골칫거리
If you have a headache, you have a pain in your head.

admit [ædmít] v. 인정하다, 시인하다
If you admit that something bad, unpleasant, or embarrassing is true, you agree, often unwillingly, that it is true.

convince [kənvíns] v. 설득하다; 납득시키다, 확신시키다 (convincing a. 설득력 있는)
If you describe someone or something as convincing, you mean that they make you believe that a particular thing is true, correct, or genuine.

evidence [évədəns] n. 증거, 흔적; v. 증거가 되다, 증언하다
Evidence is anything that you see, experience, read, or are told that causes you to believe that something is true or has really happened.

championship [ʧǽmpiənʃip] n. 선수권, 챔피언 지위; 선수권 대회, 챔피언전
The championship refers to the title or status of being a sports champion.

history [hístəri] n. 역사; 역사(학)
You can refer to the events of the past as history.

coo [ku:] v. 달콤하게 속삭이다; (비둘기가) 울다; n. (비둘기의) 울음소리
When someone coos, they speak in a very soft, quiet voice which is intended to sound attractive.

doubt [daut] n. 의심, 의혹, 의문; v. 확신하지 못하다, 의심하다
If you have doubt or doubts about something, you feel uncertain about it and do not know whether it is true or possible.

sweep away idiom 완전히 없애다, 모조리 지우다
If you sweep something away, you destroy or get rid of it completely.

proof [pru:f] n. 증거; 증명(서); 입증
Proof is a fact, argument, or piece of evidence which shows that something is definitely true or definitely exists.

warn [wɔːrn] v. 경고하다, 주의를 주다; 강력히 충고하다
If you warn someone not to do something, you advise them not to do it so that they can avoid possible danger or punishment.

point [pɔint] v. (손가락 등으로) 가리키다; (길을) 알려 주다; n. 의미; 요점
If you point at a person or thing, you hold out your finger toward them in order to make someone notice them.

pitch [pitʃ] v. 투구하다; (힘껏) 내던지다; n. 정도, 강도 (pitching n. 투구)
In the game of baseball, when you pitch the ball, you throw it to the batter for them to hit it.

wave [weiv] v. 손짓하다; 흔들다; n. 파도, 물결; (팔·손·몸을) 흔들기
If you wave or wave your hand, you move your hand from side to side in the air, usually in order to say hello or goodbye to someone.

pardner [páːrdnər] n. (격식을 갖추지 않는 호칭으로) 파트너
Pardner refers to a friend or partner and it is used as a term of address.

stomach [stʌ́mək] n. 복부; 배
Your stomach is the organ inside your body where food is digested before it moves into the intestines.

flip-flop [flíp-flap] v. 덜컥덜컥 움직이다; (태도를) 갑자기 바꾸다;
n. (태도·의견 등의) 돌변
If someone or something flip-flop, they move with a flapping sound or motion.

Chapter 5

1. **Why was Arthur waiting at the Sugar Bowl?**

   A. He was waiting to meet with Francine.

   B. He was waiting to meet his baseball team.

   C. He was waiting to have ice cream with Buster.

   D. He was waiting to work on a school project with Muffy.

2. **Why did Francine say she felt like a spy?**

   A. Arthur told her to wear sunglasses.

   B. Arthur told her to make sure she wasn't followed.

   C. Arthur gave her a secret map to the Sugar Bowl.

   D. Arthur told her that she had a special mission.

3. Why did Arthur give Francine his milkshake?

A. He was feeling full.

B. He wasn't feeling well.

C. He was trying to lose weight.

D. He was trying to collect his thoughts.

4. What animal did Arthur use in his description to help Francine understand?

A. Dinosaurs

B. Dolphins

C. Aardvarks

D. Dogs

5. Why did Arthur suddenly leave the Sugar Bowl?

A. He had forgotten his wallet and didn't have any money.

B. He wanted to go play baseball with Buster in the park.

C. He saw Binky and the Brain laughing outside the window.

D. He remembered something important that he had to do at home.

Check Your Reading Speed

1분에 몇 단어를 읽는지 리딩 속도를 측정해보세요.

$$\frac{559 \ words}{reading \ time \ (\quad) \ sec} \times 60 = (\quad) \ WPM$$

Build Your Vocabulary

★ **booth** [bu:θ] n. (식당의) 칸막이된 자리; (칸막이를 한) 작은 공간
A booth in a restaurant or café consists of a table with long fixed seats on two or sometimes three sides of it.

★ **straw** [strɔ:] n. 빨대
A straw is a thin tube of paper or plastic, which you use to suck a drink into your mouth.

복습 **tie** [tai] v. (끈 등으로) 묶다; 결부시키다; n. 끈; (강한) 유대관계
If you tie two things together or tie them, you fasten them together with a knot.

복습 **knot** [nat] n. 매듭; (복부·목 등이) 뻣뻣한 느낌; v. 매듭을 묶다
If you tie a knot in a piece of string, rope, cloth, or other material, you pass one end or part of it through a loop and pull it tight.

★ **stubborn** [stʌ́bərn] a. 다루기 힘든; 완고한, 고집스러운
A stubborn stain or problem is difficult to remove or to deal with.

get out into the open idiom 밝히다; 공표하다
To get something out into the open means to tell people information that was secret.

★ **imagination** [imædʒənéiʃən] n. 상상력, 상상; 가상; 착각; 창의력
Your imagination is the ability that you have to form pictures or ideas in your mind of things that are new and exciting, or things that you have not experienced.

* **sip** [sip] n. 한 모금; v. (음료를) 조금씩 마시다 (take a sip idiom 한 모금 마시다)
A sip is a small amount of drink that you take into your mouth.

secretive [síːkritiv] a. 비밀스러운
If you are secretive, you like to have secrets and to keep your knowledge, feelings, or intentions hidden.

복습 **nod** [nad] v. (고개를) 끄덕이다, 끄덕여 나타내다; n. (고개를) 끄덕임
If you nod, you move your head downward and upward to show agreement, understanding, or approval.

double back idiom (오던 길로) 되돌아가다
If you double back on your way, you turn around and go back in the direction you have come from.

* **track** [træk] n. (이동하는) 방향; 발자국, 자국; v. 추적하다, 뒤쫓다
Track is the direction that someone or something has taken.

* **privacy** [práivəsi] n. (남의 간섭 등을 받지 않고) 혼자 있는 상태, 사생활(을 누리는 상태)
If you have privacy, you are in a place or situation which allows you to do things without other people seeing you or disturbing you.

big deal [bíg díːl] n. 대단한 것, 큰 일; int. 그게 무슨 대수라고!
If you say that something is a big deal, you mean that it is important or significant in some way.

복습 **snort** [snɔːrt] v. 코웃음을 치다, 콧방귀를 뀌다; n. 코웃음, 콧방귀
If someone snorts something, they say it in a way that shows contempt.

never mind idiom (중요하지 않으니까) 신경 쓰지 마, 괜찮아
You use 'never mind' to tell someone not to do something or worry about something, because it is not important.

* **private** [práivət] a. 혼자 있을 수 있는; 은밀한; 사유의, 개인 소유의; 사적인
(in private idiom 다른 사람이 없는 데서)
If you do something in private, you do it without other people being present, often because it is something that you want to keep secret.

breath [breθ] n. 숨, 입김 (take a deep breath idiom 심호흡하다)
When you take a deep breath, you breathe in a lot of air at one time.

satisfy [sætisfài] v. 만족시키다; 채우다 (satisfied a. 납득하는; 만족하는)
If you are satisfied that something is true or has been done properly, you are convinced about this after checking it.

eavesdrop [íːvzdrap] v. 엿듣다, 도청하다
If you eavesdrop on someone, you listen secretly to what they are saying.

overhear [òuvərhíər] v. (overheard–overheard) (남의 대화 등을) 우연히 듣다
If you overhear someone, you hear what they are saying when they are not talking to you and they do not know that you are listening.

collect [kəlékt] v. 마음을 가다듬다, (생각을) 정리하다; 모으다, 수집하다
If you collect yourself or collect your thoughts, you make an effort to calm yourself or prepare yourself mentally.

grab [græb] v. 붙잡다, 움켜잡다; n. 와락 잡아채려고 함
If you grab something, you take it or pick it up suddenly and roughly.

discuss [diskʌ́s] v. 의논하다, 논의하다; 논하다
If people discuss something, they talk about it, often in order to reach a decision.

slurp [sləːrp] v. 후루룩 마시다; 후루룩 하는 소리를 내다; n. 홀짝홀짝 마시는 소리
If you slurp a liquid, you drink it noisily.

go on idiom 말을 계속하다; (어떤 상황이) 계속되다; 시작하다
When you go on, you continue speaking after a short pause.

clasp [klæsp] v. 움켜쥐다; 껴안다; n. 움켜쥐기, 잡기; 걸쇠
If you clasp someone or something, you hold them tightly in your hands or arms.

hopeful [hóupfəl] a. 희망에 찬, 기대하는; 희망적인 (hopefully ad. 희망을 갖고)
If you are hopeful, you are fairly confident that something that you want to happen will happen.

roll one's eyes idiom 눈을 굴리다
If you roll your eyes, you move them round and upward when you are frightened, bored, or annoyed.

suppose [səpóuz] v. 가정하다; (~이라고) 생각하다, 추측하다
You can use suppose or supposing before mentioning a possible situation or action. You usually then go on to consider the effects that this situation or action might have.

dolphin [dálfin] n. [동물] 돌고래
A dolphin is a mammal which lives in the sea and looks like a large fish with a pointed mouth.

stuff [stʌf] n. 것(들), 물건; v. 채워 넣다; 쑤셔 넣다
You can use stuff to refer to things such as a substance, a collection of things, events, or ideas, or the contents of something in a general way without mentioning the thing itself by name.

tabletop [téibltàp] n. 테이블의 윗면
A table top is the flat surface on a table.

stare [stɛər] v. 빤히 쳐다보다, 응시하다; n. 빤히 쳐다보기, 응시
If you stare at someone or something, you look at them for a long time.

gaze [geiz] v. 가만히 응시하다, 바라보다; n. 응시, 시선
If you gaze at someone or something, you look steadily at them for a long time.

clutch [klʌʧ] v. (꽉) 움켜잡다; n. 움켜쥠; (세력의) 손아귀
If you clutch at something or clutch something, you hold it tightly, usually because you are afraid or anxious.

bat [bæt] v. (눈을) 깜박이다; (배트로) 공을 치다; n. (야구·크리켓의) 방망이
If you bat your eyes, you open and close your eyes quickly, in a way that is supposed to be attractive.

impatient [impéiʃənt] a. 짜증난, 안달하는; 어서 ~하고 싶어 하는
(impatiently ad. 성급하게, 조바심하며)
If you are impatient, you are annoyed because you have to wait too
long for something.

double over idiom (웃음·고통으로) 몸을 웅크리다
If you double over, you bend your body suddenly or quickly because of
pain or laughter.

race [reis] v. 쏜살같이 가다; 경쟁하다, 경주하다; n. 경주; 인종, 민족
If you race somewhere, you go there as quickly as possible.

puzzle [pʌzl] v. 어리둥절하게 하다; n. 퍼즐; 수수께끼 (puzzled a. 어리둥절해하는)
Someone who is puzzled is confused because they do not understand
something.

frown [fraun] n. 찡그림, 찌푸림; v. 얼굴을 찌푸리다
A frown is a facial expression or look characterized by a furrowing of a
person brows.

strange [streindʒ] a. 이상한; 낯선
Something that is strange is unusual or unexpected, and makes you feel
slightly nervous or afraid.

except [iksépt] v. 제외하다; prep. ~을 제외하고는, ~외에는 (exception n. 예외)
If you make a general statement, and then say that something or
someone is no exception, you are emphasizing that they are included
in that statement.

Chapter 6

1. **Why did Arthur call Buster?**

   A. He needed some advice about sports.

   B. He needed some advice about school.

   C. He needed some advice about dancing.

   D. He needed some advice about Francine.

2. **Why was it hard for Buster to tell if Arthur was serious?**

   A. Arthur always liked to trick Buster.

   B. Buster forgot to put on his serious hat.

   C. Buster didn't think Arthur sounded serious.

   D. Buster couldn't see Arthur's face over the phone.

3. What did Buster suggest Arthur do?

A. He suggested that he take Francine on a date.

B. He suggested that he try to kiss Francine.

C. He suggested that he keep away from Francine.

D. He suggested that he give Francine back her baseball glove.

4. Why did Arthur hang up the phone on Buster?

A. He was angry with Buster.

B. He was shocked by what Buster had said.

C. He had to make an urgent call to Francine.

D. He fell asleep while they were talking.

5. What did Arthur imagine happening to him?

A. He imagined himself getting cooties.

B. He imagined himself becoming a doctor.

C. He imagined himself getting married to Francine.

D. He imagined himself getting sick from his family.

$$\frac{560 \text{ words}}{\text{reading time (\quad) sec}} \times 60 = (\quad) \text{ WPM}$$

Build Your Vocabulary

advice [ædváis] n. 충고, 조언
If you give someone advice, you tell them what you think they should do in a particular situation.

gee [dʒiː] int. (놀람·감탄을 나타내어) 야, 와; (짜증스러움을 나타내어) 에이, 이런
People sometimes say gee to emphasize a reaction or remark.

spin [spin] v. 돌리다, 회전시키다; (휙) 돌아서다; n. 회전, 돌기
If something spins or if you spin it, it turns quickly around a central point.

propeller [prəpélər] n. 프로펠러, 추진기
A propeller is a device with blades which is attached to a boat or aircraft. The engine makes the propeller spin round and causes the boat or aircraft to move.

go on idiom 말을 계속하다; (어떤 상황이) 계속되다; 시작하다
When you go on, you continue speaking after a short pause.

give away idiom (비밀을) 누설하다, 드러내다
If you give something away, you show an emotion or quality that you are trying to hide.

in that case idiom 그런 경우에는, 그렇다면
You say in that case to indicate that what you are going to say is true if the possible situation that has just been mentioned actually exists.

match [mætʃ] v. 어울리다, (색깔·무늬·스타일이 서로) 맞다; 일치하다; n. 성냥; 경기, 시합
(matching a. 어울리는)
Matching is used to describe things which are of the same color or design.

glove [glʌv] n. 장갑
Gloves are pieces of clothing which cover your hands and wrists and have individual sections for each finger. You wear gloves to keep your hands warm or dry or to protect them.

mysterious [mistíəriəs] a. 이해하기 힘든; 신비한, 신비에 싸인
Someone or something that is mysterious is strange and is not known about or understood.

gulp [gʌlp] v. (공포·놀라움에 질려) 침을 꿀떡 삼키다; 꿀꺽꿀꺽 삼키다; n. 꿀꺽 마시기
If you gulp, you swallow air, often making a noise in your throat as you do so, because you are nervous or excited.

make up idiom (이야기 등을) 지어 내다; ~을 이루다, 형성하다
If you make up something, you invent something artificial or untrue, often in order to trick someone.

grader [gréidər] n. 학년생; 등급을 매기는 사람
Grader refers to a child or young person who is in a particular grade at school.

slump [slʌmp] v. 털썩 앉다; 급감하다, 급락하다; n. 급감, 폭락; 불황
If you slump somewhere, you fall or sit down there heavily, for example because you are very tired or you feel ill.

hang up idiom 전화를 끊다, 수화기를 놓다
If you hang up the phone, you end a telephone conversation, often very suddenly.

daze [deiz] n. 멍한 상태; 눈이 부심; v. 멍하게 하다; 눈부시게 하다
(in a daze idiom 어리둥절한 상태인)
If someone is in a daze, they are feeling confused and unable to think clearly, often because they have had a shock or surprise.

^{복습} **stare** [stɛər] v. 빤히 쳐다보다, 응시하다; n. 빤히 쳐다보기, 응시
If you stare at someone or something, you look at them for a long time.

[*] **ceiling** [síːliŋ] n. 천장
A ceiling is the horizontal surface that forms the top part or roof inside
a room.

[*] **examine** [igzǽmin] v. 검사하다, 진찰하다; 조사하다, 검토하다
(examination table n. 진찰대)
If a doctor examines you, he or she looks at your body, feels it, or does
simple tests in order to check how healthy you are.

[*] **shiver** [ʃívər] v. (추위·두려움·흥분 등으로 몸을) 떨다; n. 전율; 몸서리; 오한
When you shiver, your body shakes slightly because you are cold or
frightened.

[*] **cover** [kávər] v. 덮다; 씌우다, 가리다; n. (책이나 잡지의) 표지; 덮개
If one thing covers another, it forms a layer over its surface.

rash [ræʃ] n. 발진, 뾰루지; a. 경솔한, 성급한
A rash is an area of red spots that appears on your skin when you are
ill or have a bad reaction to something that you have eaten or touched.

[*] **nearby** [nìərbái] ad. 인근에, 가까운 곳에; a. 인근의, 가까운 곳의
If something is nearby, it is only a short distance away.

^{복습} **afraid** [əfréid] a. 걱정하는; 두려워하는, 겁내는
If you are afraid that something unpleasant will happen, you are worried
that it may happen and you want to avoid it.

cootie [kúːti] n. 이; 세균
Cootie is a slang name for the body louse.

[*] **rush** [rʌʃ] v. 급히 움직이다, 서두르다; 재촉하다; n. 혼잡, 분주함; (감정이) 치밀어 오름
If you rush somewhere, you go there quickly.

forward [fɔ́:rwərd] ad. 앞으로; 미래로; 더 일찍, 빨리; a. 앞으로 가는;
v. (물건·정보를) 보내다
If you move or look forward, you move or look in a direction that is in front of you.

hug [hʌg] n. 껴안기, 포옹; v. 껴안다, 포옹하다; (무엇을) 끌어안다
A hug is the act of holding someone or something close to your body with your arms.

contagious [kəntéidʒəs] a. 전염되는, 전염성의; 전염병에 걸린
A disease that is contagious can be caught by touching people or things that are infected with it.

brush [brʌʃ] v. 솔질을 하다; (솔이나 손으로) 털다; n. 붓; 솔; 비
(brush one's teeth idiom 이를 닦다, 양치질을 하다)
If you brush your teeth, you clean your teeth with toothbrush and toothpaste.

diet [dáiət] n. 식습관; 식사; 다이어트; v. 다이어트를 하다
Your diet is the type and range of food that you regularly eat.

personal [pɔ́rsənl] a. 개인의, 개인적인; 직접 한
A personal opinion, quality, or thing belongs or relates to one particular person rather than to other people.

groom [gru:m] v. 몸치장하다; 다듬다; (동물을) 손질하다; n. 마부; 신랑
(grooming n. 차림새, 몸단장)
Grooming refers to the things that people do to keep themselves clean and make their face, hair, and skin look nice.

gasp [gæsp] v. 숨이 턱 막히다, 헉 하고 숨을 쉬다; n. 헉 하는 소리를 냄
When you gasp, you take a short quick breath through your mouth, especially when you are surprised, shocked, or in pain.

lately [léitli] ad. 최근에, 얼마 전에
You use lately to describe events in the recent past, or situations that started a short time ago.

count [kaunt] v. 인정하다; (수를) 세다; 계산하다; n. 셈, 계산; 수치
If something counts or is counted as a particular thing, it is regarded as being that thing, especially in particular circumstances or under particular rules.

honest [ánist] ad. 진정으로; a. 솔직한; 정직한
You say 'honest' before or after a statement to emphasize that you are telling the truth and that you want people to believe you.

cure [kjuər] n. 치유하는 약, 치유법; 해결책; v. 낫게 하다; 치유하다; 해결하다
A cure for an illness is a medicine or other treatment that cures the illness.

technology [teknálədʒi] n. (과학) 기술; 기계, 장비 (technological a. (과학) 기술적인)
Technology refers to methods, systems, and devices which are the result of scientific knowledge being used for practical purposes.

wonder [wʌ́ndər] n. 경탄, 경이; v. 궁금해하다; (크게) 놀라다
A wonder is something that causes people to feel great surprise or admiration.

sigh [sai] v. 한숨을 쉬다, 한숨짓다; n. 한숨; 탄식
When you sigh, you let out a deep breath, as a way of expressing feelings such as disappointment, tiredness, or pleasure.

reach [riːʃ] n. 범위; 거리; v. (손·팔을) 뻗다, 내밀다; 이르다, 도달하다
Someone's or something's reach is the distance or limit to which they can stretch, extend, or travel.

medical [médikəl] a. 의학의, 의료의
Medical means relating to illness and injuries and to their treatment or prevention.

doom [duːm] v. 불행한 운명을 맞게 하다; n. 죽음, 파멸 (doomed a. 운이 다한, 불운한)
If something is doomed to happen, or if you are doomed to a particular state, something unpleasant is certain to happen, and you can do nothing to prevent it.

Chapter 7

1. **What did Arthur's father tell him about feeling like not going to school?**

   A. Arthur's father told him that it wasn't a problem on rainy days.

   B. Arthur's father told him that it always happened on big test days.

   C. Arthur's father told him that he could pretend to be sick and stay home.

   D. Arthur's father told him that he never felt that when when he was young.

2. **How was Arthur playing with his food at breakfast?**

   A. He was tossing his food at D.W.

   B. He put his bacon into the shape of a heart.

   C. He cut his pancake into the shape of a heart.

   D. He put his scrambled eggs into the shape of a heart.

3. **What did D.W.'s teacher say it was good to be?**
   A. Smart
   B. Curious
   C. Lovely
   D. Friendly

4. **Why did Arthur brush off his shoulder where Francine had touched him?**
   A. It had gotten dirty from her hand.
   B. He wanted his clothes to look nice in class.
   C. He thought that it would bring him good luck.
   D. He didn't want to take any chances with cooties.

5. **What did Arthur almost do while saying it was a joke?**
   A. He almost walked into a closed door.
   B. He almost walked out of the school.
   C. He almost walked into the staff room.
   D. He almost walked into the girls' bathroom.

Check Your Reading Speed

1분에 몇 단어를 읽는지 리딩 속도를 측정해보세요.

$$\frac{506 \ words}{reading \ time \ (\quad) \ sec} \times 60 = (\quad) \ WPM$$

Build Your Vocabulary

c'mon idiom (= come on) 서둘러, 빨리; 자 어때

You use 'c'mon' to encourage someone do something, for example, to hurry.

peer [piər] v. 유심히 보다, 눈여겨보다; n. 동료, 또래

If you peer at something, you look at it very hard, usually because it is difficult to see clearly.

unfortunate [ʌnfɔ́ːrʃənət] a. 유감스러운; 불운한, 불행한

(unfortunately ad. 불행하게도, 유감스럽게도)

You can use unfortunately to introduce or refer to a statement when you consider that it is sad or disappointing, or when you want to express regret.

cootie [kúːti] n. 이; 세균

Cooties is a slang name for the body louse.

nod [nad] v. (고개를) 끄덕이다, 끄덕여 나타내다; n. (고개를) 끄덕임

If you nod, you move your head downward and upward to show agreement, understanding, or approval.

glance [glæns] v. 흘깃 보다; 대충 훑어보다; n. 흘깃 봄

If you glance at something or someone, you look at them very quickly and then look away again immediately.

groan [groun] v. 신음 소리를 내다, 끙끙거리다; n. 신음, 끙 하는 소리
If you groan, you make a long, low sound because you are in pain, or because you are upset or unhappy about something.

make it idiom 가다; 버텨 내다; 성공하다; 이겨내다
If you make it somewhere, you succeed in reaching there.

point [pɔint] v. (손가락 등으로) 가리키다; (길을) 알려 주다; n. 의미; 요점
If you point at a person or thing, you hold out your finger toward them in order to make someone notice them.

plate [pleit] n. 접시, 그릇; (자동차) 번호판; 판, 패 v. 판을 대다
A plate is a round or oval flat dish that is used to hold food.

rearrange [rìːəréindʒ] v. 재배열하다; (몸의 자세를) 바꾸다; 재조정하다
If you rearrange things, you change the way in which they are organized or ordered.

scramble [skræmbl] v. (달걀을 휘저어) 스크램블을 만들다; 재빨리 움직이다; n. (힘들게) 기어가기
If you scramble eggs, you break them, mix them together and then heat and stir the mixture in a pan.

imagination [imædʒənéiʃən] n. 상상력, 상상; 착각, 가상; 창의력
Your imagination is the part of your mind which allows you to form pictures or ideas of things that do not necessarily exist in real life.

hasty [héisti] a. 서두른, 성급한; 경솔한 (hastily ad. 급히, 허둥지둥)
A hasty movement, action, or statement is sudden, and often done in reaction to something that has just happened.

bite [bait] n. 한 입; 물기; v. (이빨로) 물다
A bite of something, especially food, is the action of biting it.

distract [distrǽkt] v. 집중이 안되게 하다, (주의를) 딴 데로 돌리다 (distracted a. 산만해진)
If you are distracted, you are not concentrating on something because you are worried or are thinking about something else.

admit [ædmít] v. 인정하다, 시인하다
If you admit that something bad, unpleasant, or embarrassing is true, you agree, often unwillingly, that it is true.

pesky [péski] a. 귀찮은, 성가신
Pesky means irritating.

curious [kjúəriəs] a. 궁금한, 호기심이 많은; 별난, 특이한
If you are curious about something, you are interested in it and want to know more about it.

face [feis] v. 대면하다; ~을 마주보다; (상황에) 직면하다; n. 얼굴; 표면
If you have to face a person or group, you have to stand or sit in front of them and talk to them, although it may be difficult and unpleasant.

gym [dʒim] n. (특히 학교에서 하는) 운동; (= gymnasium) 체육관
Gym is the activity of doing physical exercises in a gym, especially at school.

locker [lákər] n. (자물쇠가 달린) 사물함
A locker is a small metal or wooden cupboard with a lock, where you can put your personal possessions.

tap [tæp] v. (가볍게) 톡톡 두드리다; n. (가볍게) 두드리기; 수도꼭지
If you tap something, you hit it with a quick light blow or a series of quick light blows.

bit [bit] n. 조금, 약간; 조각
A bit means to a small extent or degree. It is sometimes used to make a statement less extreme.

jumpy [dʒʌ́mpi] a. 조마조마한
If you are jumpy, you are nervous or worried about something.

ride [raid] n. (차량·자전거 등을) 타고 달리기; 여정; v. (자전거·오토바이·말 등을) 타다
A ride is a journey on a horse or bicycle, or in a vehicle.

weird [wiərd] a. 기이한, 기묘한; 기괴한, 섬뜩한
If you describe something or someone as weird, you mean that they are strange.

brush [brʌʃ] v. (솔이나 손으로) 털다; 솔질을 하다; n. 붓; 솔; 비
If you brush something somewhere, you remove it with quick light movements of your hands.

take a chance idiom ~을 운에 맡기고 해보다; ~의 기회를 이용하다
When you take a chance, you try to do something although there is a large risk of danger or failure.

give a look idiom ~를 보다; 표정을 짓다
If you give someone a look, you look at them in a particular way.

super [súːpər] a. 대단한, 굉장히 좋은; ad. 특별히
Some people use super to mean very nice or very good.

hall [hɔːl] n. (건물 안의) 복도; 현관; 넓은 방, 홀
A hall in a building is a long passage with doors into rooms on both sides of it.

strange [streindʒ] a. 이상한; 낯선
Something that is strange is unusual or unexpected, and makes you feel slightly nervous or afraid.

silly [síli] a. 어리석은, 바보 같은; 유치한; n. 바보
If you say that someone or something is silly, you mean that they are foolish, childish, or ridiculous.

nervous [nə́ːrvəs] a. 불안해하는, 초조해하는; 겁을 잘 먹는
If someone is nervous, they are frightened or worried about something that is happening or might happen, and show this in their behavior.

be about to idiom 막 ~하려던 참이다
If you are about to do something, you are going to do it very soon.

jerk [dʒəːrk] v. 홱 움직이다; n. (갑자기 날카롭게) 홱 움직임; 얼간이

If you jerk something or someone in a particular direction, or they jerk in a particular direction, they move a short distance very suddenly and quickly.

joke [dʒouk] n. 우스개, 농담; v. 농담하다, 재미있는 이야기를 하다

A joke is something that is said or done to make you laugh, for example a funny story.

concern [kənsə́ːrn] v. ~를 걱정스럽게 만들다; 영향을 미치다; n. 우려; 염려

(as far as one is concerned idiom 개인적으로는)

You can say 'as far as I'm concerned' to indicate that you are giving your own opinion.

Chapter 8

1. Why did Arthur sit at a table of fourth graders?

    A. He needed their help with a problem about girls.

    B. He wanted to be in the fourth grade.

    C. He was trying to avoid Francine.

    D. He thought that they would be nicer.

2. What did the fourth graders call Arthur?

    A. A baby

    B. A bug

    C. A little boy

    D. A friend

3. Why did Francine come over to Arthur?

A. She told him to meet her after lunch.

B. She told him to stop talking with her.

C. She told him that she had saved him a seat.

D. She told him that she had another surprise for him.

4. What did Arthur tell the fourth graders about Francine?

A. Arthur told them that she was a friend.

B. Arthur told them that she was his girlfriend.

C. Arthur told them that she was in the same class as him.

D. Arthur told them that she always ate lunch with him.

5. What did Prunella tell Francine to do about Arthur?

A. Prunella told her to make excuses to get away.

B. Prunella told her to hesitate when she talked to him.

C. Prunella told her to tell Arthur that she didn't love him.

D. Prunella told her to tell Arthur that she was a little ahead of herself.

Check Your Reading Speed

1분에 몇 단어를 읽는지 리딩 속도를 측정해보세요.

$$\frac{500 \text{ words}}{\text{reading time ( ) sec}} \times 60 = (\quad) \text{ WPM}$$

Build Your Vocabulary

strange [streindʒ] a. 이상한; 낯선
Something that is strange is unusual or unexpected, and makes you feel slightly nervous or afraid.

save a seat idiom 자리를 마련하다, 자리를 맡다
If you save a seat for someone, you try and hold a spot or chair for them at a public place.

wave [weiv] v. 손짓하다; 흔들다; n. 파도, 물결; (팔·손·몸을) 흔들기
If you wave or wave your hand, you move your hand from side to side in the air, usually in order to say hello or goodbye to someone.

crowd [kraud] v. 가득 메우다; (생각이 마음속에) 밀려오다; n. 사람들, 군중, 무리
(crowded a. 붐비는, 복잡한)
If a place is crowded, it is full of people.

cafeteria [kæfətíəriə] n. 구내식당
A cafeteria is a restaurant where you choose your food from a counter and take it to your table after paying for it.

pretend [priténd] v. ~인 척하다, 가식적으로 행동하다; ~라고 상상하다; a. 가짜의
If you pretend that something is the case, you act in a way that is intended to make people believe that it is the case, although in fact it is not.

grader [gréidər] n. 학년생; 등급을 매기는 사람
Grader refers to a child or young person who is in a particular grade at school.

reluctant [rilʌ́ktənt] a. 꺼리는, 마지못한, 주저하는
(reluctantly ad. 마지못해서, 꺼려하여)
If you are reluctant to do something, you are unwilling to do it and hesitate before doing it, or do it slowly and without enthusiasm.

make room for idiom ~을 위해 자리를 비키다, 자리를 양보하다
If you make room for someone, you provide space for them.

ignore [ignɔ́:r] v. 무시하다, 못 본 척하다
If you ignore someone or something, you pay no attention to them.

buzz off idiom 저리가, 꺼져
When you say 'buzz off' to someone, you tell them, not very politely, to go away.

attention [əténʃən] n. 주의, 주목; 관심 (pay attention idiom 주의를 기울이다)
If you pay attention to someone, you watch them, listen to them, or take notice of them.

snicker [sníkər] v. 낄낄 웃다, 숨죽여 웃다; n. 낄낄 웃음, 숨죽여 웃는 웃음
If you snicker, you laugh quietly in a disrespectful way, for example at something rude or embarrassing.

hip [hip] n. 허리; 둔부, 엉덩이
Your hips are the two areas at the sides of your body between the tops of your legs and your waist.

sharp [ʃa:rp] a. (커브 등이) 급격한; (칼날 등이) 날카로운 (sharply ad. 급격히)
A sharp bend or turn is one that changes direction suddenly.

rest [rest] n. 나머지 (사람들·것들); 휴식; v. 쉬다; 기대다
The rest is used to refer to all the parts of something or all the things in a group that remain or that you have not already mentioned.

make sense idiom 의미가 통하다, 이해가 되다; 타당하다
If something makes sense, you can understand it.

stare [stɛər] v. 빤히 쳐다보다, 응시하다; n. 빤히 쳐다보기, 응시
If you stare at someone or something, you look at them for a long time.

matter [mǽtər] n. 문제, 일; 물질; 상황; v. 중요하다; 문제되다

You use matter in expressions such as 'What's the matter?' or 'Is anything the matter?' when you think that someone has a problem and you want to know what it is.

excuse [ikskjúːz] n. 변명, 이유; 핑계 거리; v. 용서하다; 변명하다; 양해를 구하다

An excuse is a reason which you give in order to explain why something has been done or has not been done, or in order to avoid doing something.

get away idiom 도망치다; (~로부터) 벗어나다

If you get away from someone or some place, you escape from them or there.

except [iksépt] prep. ~을 제외하고는, ~외에는; v. 제외하다

You use except to introduce the only thing or person that a statement does not apply to, or a fact that prevents a statement from being completely true.

insist [insíst] v. 고집하다, 주장하다, 우기다

If you insist that something should be done, you say so very firmly and refuse to give in about it.

private [práivət] a. 혼자 있을 수 있는; 은밀한; 사유의, 개인 소유의; 사적인

(in private idiom 다른 사람이 없는 데서)

If you do something in private, you do it without other people being present, often because it is something that you want to keep secret.

cheek [ʧiːk] n. 볼, 뺨

Your cheeks are the sides of your face below your eyes.

hesitate [hézətèit] v. 망설이다, 주저하다; 거리끼다

If you hesitate, you do not speak or act for a short time, usually because you are uncertain, embarrassed, or worried about what you are going to say or do.

nod [nad] v. (고개를) 끄덕이다, 끄덕여 나타내다; n. (고개를) 끄덕임

If you nod, you move your head downward and upward to show agreement, understanding, or approval.

ridiculous [ridíkjuləs] a. 말도 안 되는, 터무니없는, 웃기는
If you say that something or someone is ridiculous, you mean that they are very foolish.

shrug [ʃrʌg] v. (어깨를) 으쓱하다; n. (어깨를) 으쓱하기
If you shrug, you raise your shoulders to show that you are not interested in something or that you do not know or care about something.

sign [sain] n. 징후, 흔적; 몸짓; v. 서명하다; 신호를 보내다
If there is a sign of something, there is something which shows that it exists or is happening.

make a face idiom 얼굴을 찌푸리다; 침울한 표정을 짓다
If you make a face, you show a feeling such as dislike or disgust by putting an exaggerated expression on your face.

gross [grous] a. 역겨운; 아주 무례한
If you describe something as gross, you think it is very unpleasant.

be ahead of oneself idiom 앞서다; 앞지르다; 선행하다
If you are ahead of yourself, you do or say something sooner than it ought to be done.

irresistible [irizístəbl] a. (너무 매력적이어서) 거부할 수가 없는; 저항할 수 없는
If you describe something or someone as irresistible, you mean that they are so good or attractive that you cannot stop yourself from liking them or wanting them.

sigh [sai] v. 한숨을 쉬다, 한숨짓다; n. 한숨; 탄식
When you sigh, you let out a deep breath, as a way of expressing feelings such as disappointment, tiredness, or pleasure.

burden [bəːrdn] n. 부담, 짐; v. 부담을 지우다; (무거운) 짐을 나르다
If you describe a problem or a responsibility as a burden, you mean that it causes someone a lot of difficulty, worry, or hard work.

responsible [rispánsəbl] a. 책임이 있는, 책임지고 있는; 책임감 있는
(responsibility n. 책임, 의무)
If you have responsibility for something or someone, or if they are your responsibility, it is your job or duty to deal with them and to take decisions relating to them.

break one's heart idiom ~를 비통하게 만들다, ~의 가슴을 찢어 놓다
If someone breaks your heart, they make you very sad and unhappy, usually because they end a love affair or close relationship with you.

delicate [délikət] a. 미묘한, 까다로운; 연약한, 부서지기 쉬운; 정교한
You use delicate to describe a situation, problem, matter, or discussion that needs to be dealt with carefully and sensitively in order to avoid upsetting things or offending people.

plate [pleit] n. 접시, 그릇; (자동차) 번호판; 판, 패 v. 판을 대다
A plate is a round or oval flat dish that is used to hold food.

gentle [dʒentl] a. 온화한, 순한; 조용한, 조심스러운; 가벼운, 순한
Someone who is gentle is kind, mild, and calm.

Chapter 9

1. **What did Francine and Arthur think they should NOT do?**
   A. Go to the same school
   B. Dance with each other
   C. Skip gym class
   D. Be seen together

2. **Who did Arthur choose for a partner?**
   A. Francine
   B. Muffy
   C. Prunella
   D. Binky

3. **Why did Arthur turn his head toward Binky and Francine as they passed?**

   A. He wanted to see how they were doing.

   B. He wanted to see if Binky would step on Francine's feet.

   C. He wanted to see if Binky would improve with Francine.

   D. He wanted to see if Francine would be jealous of him dancing with Muffy.

4. **What did Arthur miss about Francine's dancing compared to Muffy?**

   A. Francine was always careful with her steps.

   B. Francine did the right steps at the right time.

   C. Francine had better fashion sense than Muffy.

   D. Francine had more enthusiasm for square dancing.

5. **What did Arthur and Francine both say together?**

   A. "Quit trying to dance with me."

   B. "What are you doing here?"

   C. "I'm not in love with you."

   D. "I'm not trying to dance with you."

Check Your Reading Speed

1분에 몇 단어를 읽는지 리딩 속도를 측정해보세요.

$$\frac{518 \text{ words}}{\text{reading time (\quad) sec}} \times 60 = (\quad) \text{ WPM}$$

Build Your Vocabulary

gym [dʒim] n. (= gymnasium) 체육관; (특히 학교에서 하는) 운동
A gym is a club, building, or large room, usually containing special equipment, where people go to do physical exercise and get fit.

motion [móuʃən] n. 움직임; 동작, 몸짓; v. 몸짓을 해 보이다
Motion is the activity or process of continually changing position or moving from one place to another.

clammy [klǽmi] a. (기분 나쁘게) 축축한
Something that is clammy is unpleasantly damp or sticky.

sweat [swet] n. 땀; v. 땀을 흘리다; 물기가 스며 나오다
Sweat is the salty colorless liquid which comes through your skin when you are hot, ill, or afraid.

gather [gǽðər] v. (여기 저기 있는 것을) 모으다; (사람들이) 모이다
If you gather things, you collect them together so that you can use them.

forehead [fɔ́ːrhèd] n. 이마
Your forehead is the area at the front of your head between your eyebrows and your hair.

crystal ball [krístl bɔ́ːl] n. (점칠 때 쓰는) 수정 구슬
If you say that someone, especially an expert, looks into a crystal ball, you mean that they are trying to predict the future.

predict [pridíkt] v. 예측하다, 예견하다
If you predict an event, you say that it will happen.

disaster [dizǽstər] n. 엄청난 불행, 재앙; 참사, 재난
If you refer to something as a disaster, you are emphasizing that you think it is extremely bad or unacceptable.

expect [ikspékt] v. 예상하다, 기대하다; 요구하다
If you expect something to happen, you believe that it will happen.

prepare [pripέər] v. 준비하다; 대비하다, 각오하다
If you prepare something, you make it ready for something that is going to happen.

lead [li:d] ① v. 이끌다; 지휘하다; 선두를 달리다; n. 선두, 우세 ② n. [광물] 납
If you lead a group of people, an organization, or an activity, you are in control or in charge of the people or the activity.

nervous [nə́:rvəs] a. 불안해하는, 초조해하는; 겁을 잘 먹는
(nervously ad. 신경질적으로, 초조하게)
If someone is nervous, they are frightened or worried about something that is happening or might happen, and show this in their behavior.

face [feis] v. ~을 마주보다; 대면하다; (상황에) 직면하다; n. 얼굴; 표면
If someone or something faces a particular thing, person, or direction, they are positioned opposite them or are looking in that direction.

hesitate [hézətèit] v. 망설이다, 주저하다; 거리끼다
If you hesitate, you do not speak or act for a short time, usually because you are uncertain, embarrassed, or worried about what you are going to say or do.

relieve [rilí:v] v. 안도하게 하다; (불쾌감·고통 등을) 없애 주다; 완화하다
(relieved a. 안도하는)
If you are relieved, you feel happy because something unpleasant has not happened or is no longer happening.

pair [pεər] v. (둘씩) 짝을 짓다; n. 짝, 두 사람; 한 쌍 (pair off idiom ~와 짝을 짓다)
If you pair off some people or things, you arrange them in groups of two.

* **bow** [bau] ① v. (허리를 굽혀) 절하다; (고개를) 숙이다; n. (고개 숙여 하는) 인사, 절 ② n. 활

When you bow to someone, you briefly bend your body toward them as a formal way of greeting them or showing respect.

* **smooth** [smuːð] a. 순조로운; 매끈한; 부드러운; v. 매끈하게 하다, 반듯하게 펴다 (smoothly ad. 순조롭게)

You use smooth to describe something that is going well and is free of problems or trouble.

* **except** [iksépt] prep. ~을 제외하고는, ~외에는; v. 제외하다

You use except to introduce the only thing or person that a statement does not apply to, or a fact that prevents a statement from being completely true.

* **bend** [bend] v. (bent-bent) 굽히다, 숙이다; 구부리다; n. 굽이, 굽은 곳

When you bend, you move the top part of your body downward and forward.

* **knock** [nak] v. 치다; 부딪치다; (문을) 두드리다; n. 문 두드리는 소리; 부딪침

If you knock something, you touch or hit it roughly, especially so that it falls or moves.

* **replace** [ripléis] v. 대신하다, 대체하다; 바꾸다, 교체하다 (replacement n. 교체(품))

If you refer to the replacement of one thing by another, you mean that the second thing takes the place of the first.

* **grin** [grin] v. 활짝 웃다; n. 활짝 웃음

When you grin, you smile broadly.

* **suppose** [səpóuz] v. (~이라고) 생각하다, 추측하다; 가정하다

If you suppose that something is true, you believe that it is probably true, because of other things that you know.

* **attention** [əténʃən] n. 주의, 주목; 관심 (pay attention idiom 주의를 기울이다)

If you pay attention to someone, you watch them, listen to them, or take notice of them.

˟clap [klæp] v. 손뼉을 치다; 박수를 치다; n. 박수, 손뼉

When you clap, you hit your hands together to show appreciation or attract attention.

˟arm-in-arm idiom 서로 팔짱을 끼고

If two people are walking arm in arm, they are walking together with their arms linked.

˟jealous [dʒéləs] a. 질투하는; 시기하는, 시샘하는

If someone is jealous, they feel angry or bitter because they think that another person is trying to take a lover or friend, or a possession, away from them.

fall behind idiom 뒤지다, 뒤떨어지다

If you fall behind, you fail to do something fast enough or on time.

˟jerk [dʒəːrk] v. 홱 움직이다; n. (갑자기 날카롭게) 홱 움직임; 얼간이

If you jerk something or someone in a particular direction, or they jerk in a particular direction, they move a short distance very suddenly and quickly.

˟forward [fɔ́ːrwərd] ad. 앞으로; 미래로; 더 일찍, 빨리; a. 앞으로 가는; v. (물건·정보를) 보내다

If you move or look forward, you move or look in a direction that is in front of you.

˟concentrate [kánsəntrèit] v. (정신을) 집중하다; 농축하다; n. 농축물

If you concentrate on something, you give all your attention to it.

˟enthusiasm [inθúːziæzm] n. 열정, 열의

Enthusiasm is great eagerness to be involved in a particular activity which you like and enjoy or which you think is important.

˟whisper [hwíspər] v. 속삭이다, 소곤거리다; n. 속삭임, 소곤거리는 소리

When you whisper, you say something very quietly.

stomp [stamp] v. 발을 구르며 춤추다; 쿵쿵거리며 걷다

If you stomp somewhere, you walk there with very heavy steps, often because you are angry.

yell [jel] v. 소리치다, 외치다; n. 고함, 외침
If you yell, you shout loudly, usually because you are excited, angry, or in pain.

thread [θred] v. (실 등을) 꿰다; 엮다; 요리조리 빠져나가다; n. 실; (이야기 등의) 맥락
When you thread a needle, you put a piece of thread through the hole in the top of the needle in order to sew with it.

needle [niːdl] n. 바늘
A needle is a small, very thin piece of polished metal which is used for sewing. It has a sharp point at one end and a hole in the other for a thread to go through.

form [fɔːrm] v. 형성되다, 구성하다; n. 모습, 형체; 종류; 방식
When a particular shape forms or is formed, people or things move or are arranged so that this shape is made.

row [rou] n. 열, 줄; 노 젓기; v. 노를 젓다
A row of things or people is a number of them arranged in a line.

tunnel [tʌnl] n. 터널, 굴; v. 굴을 뚫다
A tunnel is a long passage which has been made under the ground, usually through a hill or under the sea.

jostle [dʒasl] v. 거칠게 밀치다; 밀치고 나아가다; n. 혼잡
If people jostle you, they bump against you or push you in a way that annoys you, usually because you are in a crowd.

face-to-face idiom 서로 얼굴을 맞대고
If you come face to face with someone, you meet them and can talk to them or look at them directly.

hand-in-hand idiom 서로 손을 잡고
If two people are hand in hand, they are holding each other's nearest hand, usually while they are walking or sitting together.

spell out idiom ~을 자세히 설명하다; 철자를 말하다
If you spell something out, you make it clear and easy to understand or explain it in detail.

^{복습}**breath** [breθ] n. 숨, 입김 (take a deep breath idiom 심호흡하다)
When you take a deep breath, you breathe in a lot of air at one time.

Chapter

10

1. **Who was the first one to break the silence?**

   A. Arthur

   B. Francine

   C. Prunella

   D. Mrs. MacGrady

2. **What did Arthur say that he would rather have than kiss Francine?**

   A. A cold

   B. Cooties

   C. Head lice

   D. Acne

3. How did Arthur and Francine react to the dance ending and everyone staring at them?

   A. They were so embarrassed that they ran away.

   B. They realized that they would have to start dancing again.

   C. They realized the whole thing was ridiculous and burst out laughing.

   D. They thought that they should try dancing with other partners more often.

4. What did Arthur say they would not let get between Francine and him again?

   A. Love

   B. Lies

   C. Jealousy

   D. Embarrassment

5. What did Arthur and Francine do after they made up?

   A. They decided to switch dance partners with Muffy and Binky.

   B. They stopped dancing and played baseball instead.

   C. They went to go get the matching cowboy hats.

   D. They danced like crazy until the bell rang.

Check Your Reading Speed

1분에 몇 단어를 읽는지 리딩 속도를 측정해보세요.

$$\frac{295 \ words}{reading \ time \ (\qquad) \ sec} \times 60 = (\qquad) \ WPM$$

Build Your Vocabulary

★ **stun** [stʌn] v. 놀라게 하다, 아연하게 하다; 기절시키다 (stunned a. 어리벙벙한)
If you are stunned by something, you are extremely shocked or surprised by it and are therefore unable to speak or do anything.

복습 **face** [feis] v. ~을 마주보다; (상황에) 직면하다; 대면하다; n. 얼굴; 표면
If someone or something faces a particular thing, person, or direction, they are positioned opposite them or are looking in that direction.

open-mouthed [oupən-máuðd] a. (놀람·충격으로) 입이 떡 벌어진
If someone is looking open-mouthed, they are staring at something with their mouth wide open because it has shocked, frightened, or excited them.

find one's voice idiom (놀란 다음에) 말을 할 수 있게 되다
If you find your voice, you are finally able to speak after being too nervous or shy to do so.

★ **crush** [krʌʃ] n. 강렬한 사랑, 홀딱 반함; v. 으스러뜨리다; (작은 공간에) 밀어 넣다
(have a crush on idiom ~에게 홀딱 반하다)
If you have a crush on someone, you are in love with them but do not have a relationship with them.

★ **snap** [snæp] v. 딱 (하고) 움직이다; (화난 목소리로) 딱딱거리다; n. 찰칵 하는 소리
If you snap something into a particular position, or if it snaps into that position, it moves quickly into that position, with a sharp sound.

no way idiom 말도 안돼; 절대로 안 돼, 싫어
You can say no way as an emphatic way of saying no.

frown [fraun] v. 얼굴을 찌푸리다; n. 찡그림, 찌푸림
When someone frowns, their eyebrows become drawn together, because they are annoyed or puzzled.

louse [laus] n. (pl. lice) [곤충] 이
Lice are small insects that live on the bodies of people or animals and bite them in order to feed off their blood.

gross [grous] a. 역겨운; 아주 무례한
If you describe something as gross, you think it is very unpleasant.

nearby [nìərbái] ad. 인근에, 가까운 곳에; a. 인근의, 가까운 곳의
If something is nearby, it is only a short distance away.

realize [ríːəlàiz] v. 깨닫다, 알아차리다; 실현하다
If you realize that something is true, you become aware of that fact or understand it.

stare [stɛər] v. 빤히 쳐다보다, 응시하다; n. 빤히 쳐다보기, 응시
If you stare at someone or something, you look at them for a long time.

embarrass [imbǽrəs] v. 당황스럽게 하다, 쑥스럽게 하다; 곤란하게 하다
(embarrassing a. 난처한, 쑥스러운)
Something that is embarrassing makes you feel shy or ashamed.

ridiculous [ridíkjuləs] a. 말도 안 되는, 터무니없는, 웃기는
If you say that something or someone is ridiculous, you mean that they are very foolish.

burst [bəːrst] v. (burst–burst) 터지다, 파열하다; 불쑥 움직이다;
n. (갑자기) 한바탕 ～을 함 (burst out idiom 갑자기 ～하기 시작하다)
If you burst out doing something, you suddenly start doing it.

positive [pázətiv] a. 확신하는; 긍정적인; 분명한, 결정적인; n. 긍정적인 것
If you are positive about something, you are completely sure about it.

stammer [stǽmər] v. 말을 더듬다; n. 말 더듬기
If you stammer, you speak with difficulty, hesitating and repeating words or sounds.

grab [græb] v. 붙잡다, 움켜잡다; n. 와락 잡아채려고 함
If you grab something, you take it or pick it up suddenly and roughly.

bow [bau] ① n. (고개 숙여 하는) 인사, 절; v. (허리를 굽혀) 절하다; (고개를) 숙이다
② n. 활
When you make a bow, you bend the head or body or knee as a sign of reverence or submission or shame or greeting.

curtsy [kə́:rtsi] v. 무릎을 굽혀 인사하다; n. (무릎을 약간 구부리며 하는) 절
If a woman or a girl curtsies, she lowers her body briefly, bending her knees and sometimes holding her skirt with both hands, as a way of showing respect for an important person.

sigh [sai] n. 한숨; 탄식; v. 한숨을 쉬다, 한숨짓다
A sigh is a long, deep audible exhalation expressing sadness, relief, or tiredness.

skip [skip] v. 깡충깡충 뛰다; 건너뛰다; 생략하다; n. 깡충깡충 뛰기
If you skip along, you move almost as if you are dancing, with a series of little jumps from one foot to the other.

grin [grin] v. 활짝 웃다; n. 활짝 웃음
When you grin, you smile broadly.

silly [síli] a. 어리석은, 바보 같은; 유치한; n. 바보
If you say that someone or something is silly, you mean that they are foolish, childish, or ridiculous.

say a mouthful idiom (단 몇 마디 단어로) 중요한 말을 하다
To say a mouthful means to say something that is true and important using only a few words.

pardner [páːrdnər] n. (격식을 갖추지 않는 말·글에서) 파트너
Pardner refers to a friend or partner and it is used as a term of address.

rest [rest] n. 나머지 (사람들·것들); 휴식; v. 쉬다; 기대다
The rest is used to refer to all the parts of something or all the things in a group that remain or that you have not already mentioned.

folk [fouk] n. 사람들; 여러분, 얘들아; a. 민속의, 전통적인
You can refer to people as folk or folks.

raise [reiz] v. 불러일으키다, 자아내다; 들어올리다, 들다
If you raise something such as some dust, you cause to rise or form it.

dust [dʌst] n. 먼지, 티끌; 가루; v. 먼지를 털다; 털어 내다
Dust is the very small pieces of dirt which you find inside buildings, for example on furniture, floors, or lights.

1장

page 5

레이크우드 초등학교 밖은 비가 많이 내리고 있었습니다. 하지만 체육관 안은 쾌적하고 건조했으며, 학생들이 컨트리 음악에 맞추어 춤을 추고 있었습니다. 스퀘어댄스를 추는 것은 비 오는 날의 학교 전통이었습니다.

학교 식당을 운영하는 맥그래디 부인이, 그들의 스텝을 외치는 역할을 했습니다. 그녀는 여러 가지 스텝을 밟도록 그들을 이끌었습니다.

page 6

"여러분의 파트너를 빙글빙글 돌리세요." 그녀가 말했습니다. "그거예요! 계속 돌리세요."

아서와 프랜신은 훌륭하게 자신들의 동작을 해냈지만, 그들의 스퀘어 안에 있는 모든 짝들이 그들만큼 잘하지는 못했습니다. 빙키가 머피를 돌릴 때, 그녀의 두 발은 계속 땅에서 떨어졌습니다.

"그렇게 빨리 하지 마, 빙키!" 머피가 불평했습니다. "난 헬리콥터가 아니라고."

맥그래디 부인이 손뼉을 쳤습니다. "바깥에 있는 짝들! 가운데로 오세요, 손뼉을 마주쳐요! 이제 뒤로 물러나세요!"

빙키가 머피를 그에게로 잡아당기며, 느릿느릿 앞으로 나왔습니다.

"조심해!" 그녀가 균형을 잃고 프랜신에게 부딪히면서 외쳤습니다.

"이봐!" 프랜신이 말했습니다. "조심해!"

머피는 천천히 자신의 몸을 일으켰습니다. "이건 내 잘못이 아니야." 그녀가 말했습니다. "빙키가 나를 던졌어!"

page 8

두 팔을 격하게 흔들며, 빙키가 스퀘어댄스를 추며 자기 자리로 돌아갔습니다. 그의 팔꿈치가 브레인을 쳐 한쪽으로 넘어지게 했습니다. 브레인은 수 엘렌의 발을 밟았습니다. 수 엘렌은 미끄러지면서 프랜신 위로 넘어졌습니다. 다음 순간, 그들은 모두 미끄러지고, 넘어지고, 또 무엇보다도, 불평하고 있었습니다.

맥그래디 부인은 대형 카세트 라디오를 껐습니다. "내 생각엔 오늘은 이만하면 충분한 것 같구나." 그녀가 말했습니다. "너희 모두 발 동작이 무척 빠르구나." 그녀가 빙키를 힐끗 보았습니다. "그리고 나는 나머지 사람들도 최선을 다했다는 것을 알고 있단다."

체육 수업은 그 날의 마지막 시간이었습니다. 모든 아이들은 랫번 선생님의 교실로 돌아와 종이 치기 전에 자기 물건을 챙겼습니다.

"너 뭐라고 했니?" 프랜신이 머피의 책상을 지나칠 때 그녀가 머피에게 물었습니다.

"아니야." 머피가 말했습니다.

page 9

랫번 선생님이 그들을 보내주고 난 뒤, 프랜신, 머피, 그리고 아서는 학교 운동장을 향해 갔습니다.

"너 또 그러고 있어." 프랜신이 말했습니다.

"뭘 그랬다는 거야?" 머피가 물었습니다.

"중얼거리고 있잖아." 프랜신이 팔짱을 꼈습니다. "어서, 뭐가 문제야?"

머피도 팔짱을 꼈습니다. "글쎄, 네가 꼭 알아야 하겠다면, 난 그저 오늘이 얼마나 엉망인지 말하고 있었어."

아서가 고개를 끄덕였습니다. "나도 비가 오는 건 싫어."

"아니, 그거 말고." 머피가 말했습니다. "난 춤추는 것에 대해 말하는 거야."

"아, 그거." 프랜신이 웃으며, 말했습니다. "넌 아주 바빴지. 하지만 난 빙키가 점점 좋아지고 있다고 생각해."

머피는 코웃음을 쳤습니다. "그럴지도 모르지만, 나는 아까와 같은 스퀘어 댄스에서 또다시 살아남을 수 있을지 모르겠어." 그녀의 얼굴이 갑자기 밝아졌습니다. "저기, 아서! 다음 시간에 우리가 스퀘어댄스를 할 때, 내 파트너가

되어줄래?"

아서는 어깨를 으쓱거렸습니다. "좋아." 그가 말했습니다.

page 10

"잠깐만!" 프랜신이 얼굴을 찡그리며, 말했습니다. "네가 아서랑 춤을 추면, 누가 내 파트너가 되는 거야?"

바로 그때 빙키가 그들 뒤에 있는 문으로 벌컥 나왔습니다. 그의 신발 끈은 풀려 있었고, 그는 계단을 내려오다가 발이 걸려 바닥으로 굴러 넘어졌습니다.

자신의 머리를 흔들며, 그가 잠시 후에 벌떡 일어났습니다.

"난 일부러 그런 거야." 그가 말했습니다. "그랬거나 아니면 계단이 움직인 거야."

머피는 프랜신을 향해 미소 지었습니다. "너는 파트너에 대해 궁금해하고 있었지?"

"오, 안 돼." 프랜신이 말했습니다. "내 건강 보험은 그렇게까지 좋지 않아. 난 아서랑 계속 할래."

아서는 한 친구에서 다른 친구로 번갈아 보았습니다. "내가 이것에 대해 발언권이 있니?" 그가 물었습니다.

"아니!" 프랜신이 말했습니다.

"하지만—," 머피가 주장하기 시작했습니다.

"얼른, 아서." 프랜신이 끼어들었습니다

다. "내가 집까지 태워 줄게."

page 11

프랜신은 아서를 길모퉁이로 끌고 갔고, 그곳에는 그녀의 아버지가 자신의 쓰레기 수거 트럭에서 기다리고 있었습니다. 아서는 한 번 뒤돌아보았지만, 머피의 얼굴에 떠오른 표정을 보게 되자, 다시 돌아보지 않았습니다.

2장

page 12

머피는 벤치에 앉아 한숨을 쉬었습니다. 비가 그쳤고, 해가 구름 뒤에서 빼꼼 나오고 있었지만, 소용이 없었습니다. 그녀의 기분은 여전히 좋지 않았습니다.

"아이 참, 발이 정말 아프네." 그녀가 말했습니다.

"아마 네 신발이 너무 꽉 끼는지도 몰라." 빙키가 그녀 뒤로 다가오며, 말했습니다. 그는 자기 운동화의 끈을 다시 묶었지만, 매듭 하나가 이미 다시 풀리고 있었습니다.

"이건 아주 비싼 신발이야." 머피가 설명했습니다. "그것들은 내 발을 안락한 보호막으로 감싸준다고. 상자에 그렇게 적혀 있었어."

page 13

"오." 양말을 제외하고 다른 그 어떤 것으로 자기 발을 감싸는 것을 생각해 본 적이 없는, 빙키가 말했습니다. "네 발은 뭔가 다른 이유 때문에 아픈 것이 분명해, 그럼."

"맞아." 머피가 동의했습니다. "뭔가 다른 이유―항상 내 발가락을 밟는 춤 파트너 같은 이유 말이야."

빙키가 고개를 끄덕였습니다. "배려심이 깊지 않네. 네가 아무래도 말해야겠―이봐, 그게 이유일리가 없어. 내 말은, 내가 네 춤 파트너였잖아."

"알아."

빙키는 혼란스러워 보였습니다. "하지만 난 아무것도 느끼지 못했는데."

"나도 알고 있어." 머피가 다시 말했습니다.

"흠." 빙키가 머리를 긁적이며, 말했습니다. "아무래도 나는 내 자신의 힘을 모르는 것 같아."

머피는 한숨 쉬었습니다. "괜찮아. 난 네가 최선을 다하고 있다는 것을 알아."

"그건 맞아." 빙키가 말했습니다.

page 15

"하지만 맥그래디 부인이 '당신의 파트너를 돌리세요.'라고 말할 때, 부인은 내 발이 땅에서 떨어져야 한다고 말하는 게 아니야."

"난 다른 누구도 내 방식대로 하고 있

지 않다는 것을 눈치 챘어. 난 그저 그들의 파트너들이 충분히 힘이 세지 않다고 생각했지."

머피는 일어나서 서성거리기 시작했습니다. "그건 정말로 네 잘못이 아니야, 빙키. 내가 화를 내야 할 사람은 프랜신이야."

빙키가 고개를 끄덕였습니다. "걔도 네 발가락을 밟았구나, 응." 그가 다 알고 있다는 듯이 말했습니다.

"아니, 아니야, 그녀는 춤을 잘 춰. 단지 그녀가 아서를 나와 공유하지 않아서 그래. 내 말은, 그는 그녀의 개인적인 소유물이 아니라는 거지. 그러니까 그가 누구랑 춤을 출지를 왜 그녀가 결정해야 하는 건데? 그녀가 행동하는 것을 보면, 넌 그들이 결혼이라도 했다고 생각할 거야."

"결혼했다고?" 빙키가 충격을 받아, 말했습니다. "말도 안 돼!"

머피는 자신의 눈을 굴렸습니다. "뭐, 당연히 그들은 *진짜로* 결혼한 건 아니지. 하지만 프랜신은 확실히 자기가 그를 소유한 것처럼 행동한다니까. 그리고 그녀는 나에게 손을 떼라고 말하는데 거리낌이 없었어."

page 16

"프랜신은 언제나 자기 생각을 다 말하지." 빙키가 동의했습니다. "나는 그녀가 어떤 생각을 하고 있는지 궁금해 한

적이 없었는데, 왜냐하면 그녀가 항상 내게 알려주기 때문이야. 하지만 그녀는 함께 쓰는 걸 잘한다고. 왜 그녀가 너랑 파트너를 바꾸려고 하지 않는 걸까?"

머피는 빙키를 곁눈질했습니다. "흠, 나도 궁금하네. 뭐, 나는 가봐야겠어. 난 1시간 뒤에 발레 수업이 있어." 그녀가 아래를 힐끗 내려다보았습니다. "내 발은 그걸 엄청 좋아할 거야."

머피가 그녀의 자전거를 타고 가버리는 동안, 빙키는 잠시 서서, 생각했습니다.

갑자기 그의 두 눈이 휘둥그래졌습니다. 프랜신이 아서를 내어주지 않으려는 데에는 한 가지 이유만이 가능했습니다. 그것은 또한 왜 그들이 팔짱을 끼고서 자리를 떴는지도 설명할 수 있었습니다.

"와! 아서와 프랜신이 사랑에 빠진 것 같아." 빙키는 몸을 떨었습니다. "난 속이 울렁거릴 것 같아."

3장

page 17

다음 날 아침 아서가 자전거를 타고 학교에 갈 때, 그는 여전히 전날 일에 대해 생각하고 있었습니다. 머피와 프랜신 사이에는 무슨 일이 있었고—그것만큼은

확실했습니다. 하지만, 그것은 그가 좀처럼 이해할 수 없는 것이었습니다. 물론, 이런 것들을 이해하지 않는 편이 더 안전할 때도 있습니다. 문제는 그때가 언제인지를 알아내는 것이었습니다.

빙키가 자전거 거치대에서 그를 기다리고 있었습니다.

"안녕, 빙키." 아서가 말했습니다.

"좋은 아침이야, 사랑에 빠진 소년. 네 여자 친구는 어디 있니?"

page 18

"내 뭐?"

"네 여자 친구 말이야."

아서는 팔짱을 꼈습니다. "무슨 여자 친구?" 그가 물었습니다.

"내가 너에게 약간의 힌트를 주지. 그녀의 이름 첫 글자는 *F.F.*야."

아서는 눈을 깜빡였습니다. 그는 그런 이름의 첫 글자를 가진 사람을 오직 한 명만 알았습니다. "프랜신을 말하는 건 아니지?" 그가 말했습니다.

"물론 난 그녀를 말하는 거지. 넌 네 여자 친구의 이름 첫 글자도 모르니?"

아서는 자신의 두 손을 허리에 짚었습니다. "프랜신은 내 여자 친구가 아니야! 그건 내가 이제껏 들어봤던 이야기 가운데 가장 어처구니없는 소리야."

"아, 걱정하지 마. 네 작은 비밀은 내가 안전하게 지켜줄게."

"그건 비밀이 아니야. **비밀로 할 건 아무것도 없다고!**"

page 19

빙키가 그에게 윙크했습니다. "알았어, 아서."

"아니, 넌 몰라." 아서가 말하면서, 자신의 고개를 저으며 그는 걸어가 버렸습니다. 때로는, 빙키와 언쟁을 하지 않는 것이 더 쉬웠습니다.

"**아서와 프랜신이 나무 아래에 앉아서.**" 빙키가 그를 향해 우렁차게 외쳤습니다. "**키읔-시옷-으-이... 잠깐만. 그게 *키읔-시옷-이*.... 오, 뭐, 내가 무슨 말을 하는지 알지!**"

아서는 뒤돌아보지도 않았습니다.

아서가 사물함에 도착했을 때 그는 여전히 고개를 젓고 있었습니다. 그는 사물함 세 개정도 떨어진 곳에 있는, 프랜신을 보았습니다. 그와 그녀가, 그들 두 사람이 사귄다는 생각은 우스꽝스러웠습니다. 터무니없었습니다. 바보 같았습니다. 엉뚱했습니다. 사실, 그가 멈춰서 정말로 그것에 대해 생각했을 때, 그 생각은 꽤 웃겼습니다. "이봐, 프랜신!" 그가 말했습니다. "빙키가 방금 나한테 뭐라고 했는지 들어봐. 그가 생각하기에—"

프랜신이 자기 사물함 안으로 손을 뻗었습니다. "잠깐만, 아서." 그녀가 말했습니다. "난 너를 위한 깜짝 선물이 있어. 봐!"

page 20

그녀는 카우보이모자 두 개를 꺼냈습니다. "나는 우리 집 지하실에서 그것들을 찾았어. 텍사스에 있는 내 삼촌이 작년에 그것들을 우리에게 보내줬어."

"와!" 아서가 말했습니다. "이것들은 진짜 같다."

프랜신이 고개를 끄덕였습니다. "맞아. 난 그것들이 목장에서 많은 시간을 보냈을 거라고 확신해, 작은 송아지들(dogies)을 몰면서 말이야."

"개들(doggies)이라고?"

"아니, 송아지들. 소 말이야." 프랜신이 설명했습니다. "내게 왜 그런지는 묻지 마. 어쨌든, 난 다음 스퀘어댄스 시간에 우리가 이걸 쓸 수 있을 거라고 생각했어."

그녀는 하나를 자신의 머리 위에 탁하고 얹었고 다른 하나를 아서에게 주었습니다.

"춤추시겠어요, 파트너?" 그녀가 물었습니다.

아서는 모자를 썼고 챙 끝을 살짝 잡아당겼습니다. "영광이지요, 아가씨."

page 22

그들은 웃었고 작게 빙글 돌았습니다. 아서가 돌았을 때, 그는 복도 끝에 있는 빙키를 보았습니다. 그는 브레인에게 속삭이고 있었습니다. 처음에 브레인은 충격을 받은 것처럼 보였습니다. 그러더니 그는 웃기 시작했습니다.

갑자기 아서가 도는 것을 멈췄습니다.

"으악, 파트너!" 프랜신이 말했습니다. "다음에는 숙녀에게 경고라도 약간 해주라고."

"미안해." 아서가 말했습니다. "나는, 음, 조금 어지러워져서."

"알겠어. 그나저나, 네가 나에게 말하고 싶었던 게 뭐야? 빙키에 관한 거였던 거 같은데, 내 생각엔."

"아, 그건 중요하지 않아. 다음에 말해 줄게."

그는 카우보이모자를 프랜신에게 돌려주고 서둘러 교실로 들어갔습니다.

page 23

그날 오후, 프랜신과 머피는 여자 탈의실에서 옷을 갈아입고 있었습니다. 그들은 야구를 할 준비를 하고 있었습니다.

"운동장에서 보자." 머피가 말했습니다.

"얘, 머피." 프랜신이 말했습니다. "난 오늘 길들여야 할 새 글러브를 갖고 왔어. 너 내 예전 글러브를 쓰고 싶니? 이건 최고라고!"

머피는 프랜신이 자신의 예전 글러브를 얼마나 좋아하는지 알고 있었지만, 그렇다고 해서 *그녀* 역시 그것을 좋아해야 한다는 의미는 아니었습니다.

"나는 그렇게 생각하지 않아, 프랜신. 그건 쓰던 것이잖아."

"당연히, 이건 쓰던 것이지. 바로 그 사실이 그것을 그렇게 좋게 만드는 거야! 이 글러브는 정말 멋진 경기에 함께했었다고. 이건 자석처럼 공을 잡아챈다니까."

page 24

머피는 그것을 살펴보았습니다. "내 손이 너무 작아서 아쉽다. 네 장갑이 잘 맞지 않을 것 같아."

"뭐, 그렇다면." 프랜신은 어깨를 으쓱했습니다. "그럼, 너 이걸 아서에게 전해 줄래? 난 아직 양말과 운동화를 갈아 신어야 해."

"물론이지." 머피가 말했습니다. 그녀는 자신의 손에 있는 장갑의 무게를 가늠했습니다. "어쩌면 이게 뭔가를 잡는 것을 그에게 도와줄지도 모르지."

밖에는 아서가 이미 우익수의 위치에 있었습니다. 빙키는 중견수의 자리에서 그와 가까이 서 있었습니다. 그는 자기 입술로 크게 뽀뽀하는 소리를 내었습니다.

아서는 그를 향해 돌아섰습니다. "그만해, 빙키. 내가 마지막으로 말하는데, 프랜신과 나 사이에는 아무 일도 없어."

page 25

"그래, 맞아. 너는 어제 춤추면서 내내 그녀의 손을 잡고 있었잖아."

"우리에게는 선택할 여지가 없었어. 게다가, 너 또한 머피의 손을 잡고 있었잖아."

빙키는 뽀뽀하는 소리를 내는 것을 멈추었습니다. "이봐, 잠깐만." 그가 말하기 시작했습니다.

"게다가, 만약 네가 생각한대로 내가 느낀다면, 내가 왜 너랑 언쟁하겠니?"

"그렇게 해서 내가 진실을 알지 못하도록 하려는 거지." 빙키가 의기양양하게 말했습니다.

"글쎄, 만약 네가 진실을 아는 것을 내가 원하지 않는다면, 내가 왜 네가 볼 수 있는 공개된 곳에서 그런 걸 하겠니?"

빙키는 머리가 아프기 시작했습니다. 그는 아서의 말이 꽤 설득력 있게 들린다는 것을 인정해야만 했습니다. 그가 필요한 것은 더 많은 증거였습니다.

"오, 아서!" 머피가 그에게 뛰어왔습니다. "내가 너에게 주려고 프랜신의 글러브를 가져왔어."

아서는 놀란 것처럼 보였습니다. "그녀의 특별한 글러브 말이야? 그녀가 결승전에서 이겼을 때 썼던 바로 그거?"

page 27

"맞아." 머피가 그에게 그것을 건네주었습니다. "그녀는 정말로 네가 이것을 사용하기를 원해. 여기. 한번 껴 봐."

아서는 조심스럽게 글러브를 받았습니다. 글러브 안쪽의 공에 맞았던 모든 부분은 색이 어두워져 있었습니다. 이 장갑에는 많은 역사가 있었습니다. 그는 프랜신이 그것을 그와 함께 쓰려고 한다는 것을 믿을 수가 없었습니다. 그게 아니라면...

"오오오오, 아서!" 빙키가 부드럽게 속삭였습니다. 그의 의심은 모두 사라졌습니다. 프랜신은 백만 년이 지나도 그에게는 절대로 그녀의 글러브를 쓰게 하지 않을 것이었습니다. 하지만 아서는 달라 보였습니다. 심지어, 특별했습니다. 이제 빙키는 그가 필요한 모든 증거를 가지고 있었습니다.

"그만해, 빙키." 아서가 경고했습니다.

"그만할 것도 없어, 아서." 그가 투구 마운드를 손가락으로 가리켰습니다.

아서는 그의 손가락을 따라갔습니다. 프랜신이 그곳에 서 있었습니다. 그녀는 미소 지었고 그에게 손을 흔들었습니다.

page 28

"그거 잘 맞니?" 그녀가 외쳤습니다.

아서는 장갑을 들어 올렸고 약하게 손을 흔들었습니다. "좋아." 그가 말했습니다.

프랜신이 웃었습니다. "내 파트너에게는 오직 가장 좋은 것만 줘야지!"

아서의 속이 요동쳤습니다. 설마 빙키가 맞았던 것일까요? 그는 자신이 프랜신을 사랑하지 않는다는 것을 알고 있었습니다. 하지만 만약에... 아니, 프랜신이 그를 사랑할 리 없었습니다.

아니면 그럴 수도 있을까요?

5장

page 29

아서는 슈가 볼의 칸막이가 쳐진 자리에 앉아 있었습니다. 그는 밀크셰이크를 마시고 있었고 프랜신이 도착하기를 기다리고 있었습니다. 그는 자신의 빨대에서 나온 종이를 가지고 매듭을 묶었습니다. 그리고는 그는 그것을 풀려고 했습니다. 매듭은 꿈쩍도 하지 않았습니다.

아서는 결정을 내렸습니다. 할 수 있는 최선은 모든 것을 밝히는 것이었습니다. 아마도 걱정할 것은 전혀 없을 것입니다. 그것은 모두 그의 상상에 불과할 것입니다.

아서는 자신의 밀크셰이크를 한 모금 마셨습니다. 물론, 모두 그렇다고 생각하는 것은 매우 쉬웠습니다. 그걸 믿는 것은 또 다른 이야기였습니다.

프랜신이 들어왔을 때, 그녀는 서둘러 그가 있는 칸막이가 쳐진 자리에 앉았습니다.

"안녕, 비밀스러운 남자."

"비밀스러운 남자라고?"

그녀가 고개를 끄덕였습니다. "아서, 넌 내게 여기서 만나자고 말했고 아무한테도 말하지 말라고 했잖아. 너는 내가 누군가에게 쫓기지 않는지 확실히 하고 오던 길을 되돌아가라고도 했어. 난 꼭 스파이처럼 느껴졌다고."

"알았어, 알았어, 그러니까 난 우리의 프라이버시를 원했던 거야. 그건 그렇게 큰 문제가 아니라고."

프랜신은 코웃음을 쳤습니다. "만약 그게 그렇게 큰 문제가 아니라면, 그렇다면 왜ー? 오, 신경 쓰지 마. 어쨌든, 난 여기 왔어. 그러니까, 네가 다른 사람이 없는 데서 묻고 싶었던 이 중요한 질문이 뭐야?"

아서는 깊게 숨을 들이마셨습니다. 그는 아무도 엿듣고 있지 않다고 확신했습니다. 그는 누가 엿듣는 것을 원하지 않았습니다.

"음, 프랜신…"

그는 자기 생각을 정리하려고 하면서, 자신의 밀크셰이크를 옆으로 밀었습니다.

"저기, 너 그거 다 먹을 거야?" 그녀가 물었습니다.

아서가 고개를 저었습니다.

프랜신이 새 빨대를 집어 들고 아서의 셰이크에 넣었습니다.

"자, 내가 말했던 것처럼… 우리는 아마도 이야기를 해야 할 것 같아. 프랜신?"

프랜신은 밀크셰이크를 후루룩거리며 마시고 있었습니다.

"너 잠깐 후루룩거리며 먹는 걸 멈출 수 있겠니? 난 이미 생각하는 것도 힘들단 말이야."

프랜신은 밀크셰이크를 옆으로 밀었습니다. "미안. 계속 해."

아서는 자신의 두 손을 탁자 위에서 움켜쥐었습니다. "가끔씩 두 사람은 서로를 알고 있거나, 적어도 그들은 그렇다고 생각하지. 하지만 그들은 진짜로 그들이 생각하는 것처럼 서로를 잘 알지는 못해. 내 말은, 그들 가운데 한 사람은 서로를 잘 알지도 모르지만 다른 사람은 그렇지 않을 수도 있어. 그 다른 사람은 어쩌면 이상한 생각을 하게 될지도 모르지." 그는 희망에 차서 그녀를 바라보았습니다. "이해했어?"

프랜신은 눈을 굴렸습니다. "너 농담하는 거지? 난 네가 방금 무슨 말을 했는지 전혀 모르겠어."

"좋아. 내가 다르게 말해줄게. 음, 돌고래 두 마리가 있다고 가정해 봐. 그리고 그것들은 많은 것을 함께 했어. 하지만 그것들은 모든 것에 대하여 똑같이 느끼는 것은 아니야. 그리고 어느 날 일이 생겼는데—"

그림자가 탁자 위에 드리워졌습니다. 아서는 프랜신의 어깨 너머를 보았고 빙키와 브레인이 창문 밖에 있는 것을 보았습니다. 그들은 그와 프랜신을 쳐다보고 있었습니다. 적어도 그들은 잠시 그러고 있었습니다. 그들은 아서가 자신들을 쳐다보고 있다는 것을 보자, 서로를 응시했고, 심장을 움켜잡으며, 자신들의 눈을 깜박거렸습니다. 그리고 그들은 다시 아서를 쳐다보았습니다.

"돌고래가 어떻다고, 아서?" 프랜신이 참지 못하고 물어보았습니다.

아서는 여전히 창문 밖을 쳐다보고 있었습니다. 이제 빙키와 브레인은 몸을 굽히고, 웃고 있었습니다.

갑자기 아서가 일어났습니다. "오, 아무것도 아니야! 내가 말했던 걸 다 잊어버려. 안녕."

그는 밀크셰이크에 대한 돈을 탁자 위에 던져 놓고 뒷문으로 서둘러 나갔습니다.

프랜신은 혼란스러워 보였습니다. 그녀는 자신의 얼굴을 찌푸린 채 밀크셰이크를 마저 마셨습니다. 남자애들은 가끔씩 아주 이상하게 굴었고, 아서도 예외는 아니었습니다.

6장

그날 밤 아서가 버스터에게 전화를 걸었습니다.

"난 조언이 필요해." 그가 말했습니다.

"이런, 아서, 너 심각하게 들리는데."

"그건 바로 내가 심각한 조언이 필요하기 때문이야."

"좋아. 나도 심각하게 굴게. 난 내 진지한 모자를 쓰고 프로펠러를 돌릴게."

아서는 그에게 무슨 일이 있었는지 이야기했습니다. 그가 말을 마쳤을 때, 버스터는 잠시 조용했습니다.

"너 농담하는 거지, 그렇지?" 그가 마침내 말했습니다.

"아니야, 아니야. 나도 그랬으면 좋겠지만, 정말이야."

"왜냐하면." 버스터가 계속 말했습니다. "전화상으로는 네가 농담하는지 정말 분간하기 힘들단 말이야. 내 말은, 내가 네 얼굴을 볼 수가 없잖아. 네 얼굴은 언제나 모든 걸 드러낸다고, 아서.

하지만 내가 볼 수 없으니까—"

"버스터!" 아서가 소리 질렀습니다. "날 믿어. 난 농담하는 게 아니야. 나는 아주 심각해."

"그런 경우라면." 버스터가 말했습니다. "그건 너무나..."

그가 웃기 시작했습니다.

"너랑... 프랜신이랑... 내 말은..."

"나도 그렇게 생각했어." 아서가 말했습니다. "적어도 처음에는. 우리는 그냥 좋은 춤 파트너 같았어. 하지만 그것은 그녀에게 충분하지 않았던 거야. 그녀는 똑같은 카우보이모자를 가져왔어. 그 다음엔 그녀는 내가 그녀의 오래된 야구 글러브를 쓰게 해줬다고."

버스터가 웃음을 멈추었습니다. "맞아." 그가 기억해냈습니다. 그는 그 경기에 있었습니다.

"난 그 다음에 무슨 일이 있을지 모르겠어. 네 생각엔 내가 걱정해야 할 것 같니?"

"여자애들에 대해서 알기는 어려워." 버스터가 말했습니다. "그들은 아주 신비로울 수 있거든. 아마도 넌 그녀로부터 멀리 떨어져 있는 게 좋겠다."

"내가 어떻게 그럴 수 있어?" 아서가 물었습니다. "프랜신은 내 가장 친한 친구 중 한 명이라고."

page37

"그렇지, 하지만 그녀가 너에게 키스하려고 하면 어떡해?"

아서는 침을 꿀꺽 삼켰습니다. "뭐라고?"

"여자애들이 널 좋아하면 그렇게 한다고."

"너 그거 지어낸 이야기지."

"아니, 아니야, 난 5학년 몇 명이 언젠가 점심시간에 말하는 걸 들은 적이 있어."

아서는 그의 의자에 털썩 주저앉았습니다. 그의 눈이 충격으로 휘둥그레졌습니다.

"아서!" 버스터가 외쳤습니다. "너 괜찮아, 아서?"

아서는 멍해져서 전화를 끊었습니다. 그는 자기 방으로 올라가서, 자신의 침대 위에 누웠고, 천장을 바라보았습니다.

아서는 의사 진료실에서 진료대 위에 앉아 있었습니다. 그는 떨고 있었고, 그의 몸은 붉은 발진으로 뒤덮여 있었습니다. 그의 엄마와 아빠가 가까이에 서 있었습니다. 그들은 걱정스러운 얼굴을 했습니다.

"리드 씨와 리드 부인." 의사가 말했습니다. "유감스럽게도 안 좋은 소식이 있습니다. 아드님께 이가 있습니다."

"오, 안 돼!" 리드 부인이 외쳤습니다. "내 새끼!"

그녀는 아서를 안아주기 위해 앞으로 뛰어갔습니다.

"조심하세요." 의사가 말했습니다. "그는 매우 전염성이 강합니다."

"하지만 어떻게 이런 일이 일어날 수 있는 거죠?" 리드 부인이 물었습니다. "우리는 아서가 모든 식품군에서 먹을 수 있도록 했는걸요. 그리고 그는 아침 과 저녁으로 이를 닦아요."

"이것은 식사나 개인적인 몸단장의 문제가 아닙니다." 의사가 설명했습니다. "아서는 키스를 통해서 이를 옮았습니다."

리드 부인이 헉 하고 숨을 내쉬었습니다. "아서, 그게 사실이니?"

"나도 모르겠어요." 아서가 말했습니다.

"최근에 누가 너한테 키스한 적이 있니?"

"글쎄요, 도라 할머니..."

의사가 고개를 저었습니다. "가족은 해당되지 않는단다."

아서는 멈춰서 생각했습니다. "뭐, 그렇다면, 프랜신밖에 없네요."

"그리고 이 프랜신이란 애는 누구니?" 의사가 물었습니다.

"친구요." 아서가 말했습니다. "그냥 친구예요. 정말이에요."

"치료법은 없나요?" 리드 씨가 물었습니다.

의사는 다시 고개를 저었습니다. "우리는 기술적인 경이로움의 시대에 살고 있습니다." 그가 한숨 쉬었습니다. "하지만 어떤 것들은 여전히 의료 과학이 풀 수 없는 지점에 있답니다."

끝장났다는 것이 바로 이런 것이군, 아서는 생각했습니다.

그것은 좋은 기분이 아니었습니다.

7장

다음 날 아침 아서는 천천히 일어났습니다.

"서둘러, 아서." 그의 아버지가 침실 문을 지나면서, 말했습니다. "얼른 움직이렴." 그는 한 걸음 뒤로 물러났고 그의 아들을 자세히 들여다보았습니다. "너 괜찮니?"

불행히도, 아서는 이의 공격에 대한 꿈이 아픈 것과 같지 않다는 것을 알았습니다. "괜찮아요." 그가 말했습니다. "하지만 제가 오늘 학교에 가지 않아도 된다면 좋겠어요."

리드 씨는 고개를 끄덕였습니다. "나

도 그런 날이 있었단다. 특히 날씨가 좋을 때 말이야." 그는 창 밖을 힐끗 쳐다보았습니다. "하지만 오늘은 그런 게 문제되지 않겠구나. 비가 올 것 같으니 말이다."

page 42

아서는 신음했습니다. 비. 그것은 곧 춤을 더 춘다는 것을 의미했습니다.

그가 마침내 부엌으로 내려왔을 때, 다른 모든 사람은 이미 아침을 먹고 있었습니다. 아서는 먹으려고 앉았지만, 그는 배가 그리 고프지 않았습니다.

"엄마!" 그의 여동생 D.W.가 말했습니다. "아서 오빠가 음식을 가지고 장난치고 있어요."

"나 안 그러고 있어." 아서가 말했습니다.

D.W.가 웃었습니다. "오, 정말!" 그녀가 가리키며, 말했습니다.

아서는 자신의 접시를 내려다보았습니다. 아무 생각 없이, 그는 자신의 스크램블 에그를 하트 모양으로 재배치했었습니다.

"그건 그냥 네 상상일 뿐이야." 그가 말하면서, 서둘러서 몇 입을 먹었습니다.

"넌 정말 약간 산만해 보이는구나." 그의 어머니가 아기 케이트에게 시리얼을 주면서 말했습니다.

page 43

"머릿속에 생각이 많아서요." 아서가 인정했습니다.

"어떤 거?" D.W.가 물었습니다.

"가령 너무 많은 질문을 하는 성가신 여동생들을 어떻게 해야 할지에 대해서 말이야."

D.W.는 신경 쓰지 않았습니다. "우리 선생님이 궁금해하는 것은 좋은 거라고 말씀하셨어."

아서는 한숨 쉬었습니다. "그래, 하지만 가끔씩은 모르는 게 더 나을 수도 있다는 것을 너도 알게 될 거야."

아서가 학교에 갔을 때, 그는 머피, 버스터, 수 엘렌, 그리고 브레인을 보았습니다. 그는 프랜신이 보이지 않았습니다.

아마도 그녀가 아파서 집에 있을 거야, 그는 혼잣말했습니다. 그가 그녀가 진짜로 아프거나 그러기를 바라는 것은 아니었습니다. 그는 단지 자신이 체육 시간에 그녀를 마주보기를 원하는지 확신할 수 없었던 것뿐이었습니다.

그가 막 자신의 사물함의 문을 닫고 있을 때 누군가가 그의 어깨 위를 툭툭 쳤습니다.

"아아!" 아서가 소리 질렀습니다.

"너 오늘 아침 따라 불안해하는구나, 응?" 프랜신이 말했습니다.

page 45

"오, 너였구나." 아서가 한 발자국 뒤로 물러섰습니다. "난 오늘 네가 아마도 아플 수 있다고 생각했어."

"아니야, 난 그냥 차를 타고 왔어. 나 늦잠을 잤거든. 난 어젯밤에 정말 이상한 꿈을 꿨어."

"나도 그래." 아서가 말했습니다. 그리고 그는 프랜신이 만졌던 어깨를 털었습니다. 그는 이에 대하여 많이 알지는 못했지만, 운에 맡기지 않는 편이 더 나았습니다.

프랜신이 그를 이상하게 쳐다보았습니다. "너 괜찮아?"

"괜찮아. 아주 좋아. 최고야. 훌륭해."

그는 복도를 따라 걸어가기 시작했습니다.

프랜신은 그를 따라갔습니다. "무슨 문제 있니, 아서? 너 조금 이상하게 행동하고 있어."

그는 화장실 문에 자신의 손을 가져다 댔습니다.

"문제 있냐고?" 아서가 말했습니다. "물론 아니지! 넌 뭐 때문에 그런 바보 같은 생각을 하니?"

"글쎄, 어디 보자... 너는 불안해하고 있잖아. 초조하고 말이야. 오, 그리고 네가 지금 막 여자 화장실에 들어가려고 하는 사실도 있고."

page 46

아서가 문에서 손을 홱 떼었습니다.

"아... 난 그냥 장난친 거였어. 장난이야."

"그렇다면 뭐." 프랜신이 말했습니다. 하지만 그녀가 생각하기에, 그 장난은 그리 재미있지 않았습니다.

8장

page 47

비록 아서가 이상하게 행동하고 군다고 생각했지만, 프랜신은 여전히 점심시간에 그의 자리를 맡았습니다.

"이쪽이야, 아서!" 그녀가 부르면서, 그에게 붐비는 식당의 반대편에서 그에게 손을 흔들었습니다.

아서는 그녀를 못 본 척했습니다. 그는 4학년들이 있는 식탁에 앉으려고 했습니다. 그들은 마지못해 그에게 자리를 만들어 주었습니다.

"고마워요." 아서가 말했습니다. "형들은 여기 자주 오나요?"

4학년들이 그를 무시했습니다.

"너 무슨 소리 들었어?" 그들 가운데 한 사람이 물었습니다.

page 48

"난 그게 벌레였던 것 같은데." 다른 학생이 말했습니다.

"난 그 벌레가 꺼져 버렸으면 좋겠어." 세 번째 학생이 말했습니다. "난 그게 여기 있는 게 싫어."

"이봐!"

아서가 올려다보았습니다. 프랜신이 그의 옆에 서 있었습니다.

"너 왜 여기 앉아 있어?" 그녀가 물었습니다. "내가 네 자리를 맡아 놓았단 말이야. 너 내가 손 흔드는 것 못 봤니?"

"오, 글쎄, 내가 집중하지 않았던 것 같아. 어쨌든, 난 내가 오늘 새로운 친구를 만나게 될 것 같아."

4학년들은 낄낄거렸습니다.

프랜신은 자신의 두 손을 허리에 가져갔습니다. "좋아. 마음대로 해. 난 내 점심을 먹으러 돌아갈 거야. 난 그게 식는 걸 원하지 않으니까."

그녀는 휙 하고 돌아서 떠났습니다.

아서는 탁자에 있는 나머지 사람들에게 미소 지었습니다. "그녀는 친구예요. 여자 친구나 그런 게 아니에요. 그냥 어쩌다 보니 여자인 친구 말이에요. 그건 말이 되죠, 그렇지 않나요?"

page 50

4학년들이 그를 쳐다보았습니다.

프랜신이 자신의 탁자로 돌아왔을 때, 프루넬라는 무엇인가가 잘못되었음을 알 수 있었습니다.

"무슨 일이야?" 그녀가 물었습니다.

프랜신은 고개를 저었습니다. "아서가 바로 문제야. 그는 나한테 정말 이상하게 굴고 있어."

프루넬라는 흥미로워했습니다. "어떤 식으로?"

"내가 그에게 이야기하려고 할 때마다, 그는 빠져나갈 변명을 해. 그가 내게 슈가 볼에서 그를 다른 사람들 몰래 만나야 한다고 우겼던, 어제만 제외하고 말이야."

"흠…" 프루넬라에게 생각이 떠올랐습니다. "나한테 말해 봐. 그럴 때 그의 볼이 빨개지니?"

프랜신은 생각해 보았습니다. "응, 그랬던 것 같은데."

"그리고 그가 이야기할 때 많이 망설이니?"

프랜신이 고개를 끄덕였습니다.

"뭐, 그렇다면." 프루넬라가 말했습니다. "난 무슨 일인지 알 것 같아."

page 51

"그래?"

"난 이렇게 말하고 싶지 않지만, 프랜신, 내 생각에는 아서가 너와 사랑에 빠진 것 같아."

프랜신은 거의 넘어질 뻔했습니다. **뭐라고!** 아서가? 나랑? 말도 안 돼."

프루넬라는 어깨를 으쓱했습니다. "유감이야, 하지만 그가 모든 조짐을 보이고 있어."

프랜신은 얼굴을 찌푸렸습니다. "그건 내가 여태까지 들어봤던 말 중 가장 역겨운 거야."

"그건 꽤 흔한 일이야, 정말. 주로 나이가 더 많은 남자애들한테 나타나지. 아서는 그저 조금 앞서가는 걸 수도 있어."

"왜 나야, 그런데? 내가 그토록 거부할 수가 없니?"

프루넬라는 한숨 쉬었습니다. "그건 부담이지, 나도 알아. 그리고 그 부담은 책임과 함께 하지."

"무슨 뜻이야?"

"글쎄, 너는 아서에게 진실을 말해야 해—네가 그를 좋아하지 않는다고 말이야. 하지만 너는 또한 조심해야 해. 넌 그의 마음을 상하게 하고 싶지 않으니까."

"네 말이 맞아." 프랜신이 동의했습니다.

page 52

"그건 바로 네가 느끼는 바를 말할 조용하고, 사적인 순간을 찾아야 한다는 걸 뜻해. 이건 까다로운 상황이야."

프랜신은 식당 저 편에 있는 아서를 보았습니다. 그는 마주보고 있지 않았습니다. 그는 그저 자신의 접시를 내려다보고 있었습니다.

불쌍한 애 같으니라고, 그녀는 생각했습니다. 난 그를 아주 상냥하게 대해야 하겠어.

9장

page 53

아서는 느린 동작으로 체육관에 갔습니다. 그의 두 손은 축축했고, 그의 이마에 땀이 맺히고 있었습니다. 그는 앞으로 한 시간이 엉망진창이 되리란 것을 예견하는 데 굳이 수정 구슬이 필요하지 않았습니다. 그는 그냥 알고 있었습니다.

예상한 대로, 맥그래디 부인이 춤을 추는 데에 있어 다시 모든 사람을 이끌 준비를 하고 있었습니다. 아이들은 체육관의 한 쪽 끝에 모였습니다.

아서와 프랜신은 초조하게 서로를 마주보았습니다.

"음, 우리가 여기에 있네." 아서가 말했습니다.

"그래." 프랜신이 동의했습니다. "우리 여기 있네, 좋아."

page 54

"카우보이모자가 안 보이네."

"없어." 프랜신이 말했습니다. "난 그걸 두고 온 것 같아. 난 뛰어가서 그걸 가져올 수도 있어—네가 원한다면."

"아니야, 아니야." 아서가 말했습니다. "어쨌든, 내가 생각해 봤는데."

"나도." 프랜신이 재빨리 덧붙였습니다.

"너 내가 생각했던 거랑 똑같은 걸 생각하고 있던 거야?"

"모르겠어. 넌 무슨 생각을 하고 있었는데?"

아서가 망설였습니다. "글쎄, 넌 무슨 생각하고 있었는데?"

"너 먼저 말해."

"좋아." 아서가 말했습니다. "아마 우리는 춤을 추지 않는 게—"

"서로 함께 말이지." 프랜신이 그를 대신해서 말을 끝맺었습니다.

아서는 안도한 듯 보였습니다. "맞아!" 그가 말했습니다.

"좋아." 프랜신이 말했습니다.

그들은 다른 파트너를 찾기 위해 둘러보았습니다. 아서가 머피와 짝을 이루는 동안, 프랜신은 빙키 옆에 섰습니다.

page 55

"좋아요, 카우보이와 카우걸." 맥그래디 부인이 말했습니다. "여러분이 지난번에 췄던 춤에서 얼마나 기억하고 있는지 봅시다."

그녀는 대형 카세트 라디오를 켰습니다.

"대각선 방향에 있는 사람에게 인사하고, 당신의 파트너에게 인사하세요." 그녀가 말했습니다.

모든 사람들이 순조롭게 인사했지만,

몸을 너무 많이 구부려서 자기 머리를 프랜신의 머리에 박은, 빙키만은 예외였습니다.

"악! 빙키!"

"미안해."

"이봐, 빙키." 그들이 맥그래디 부인의 다음 지시를 기다리는 동안, 프랜신이 말했습니다. "너 조심해야 해. 난 발이 두 개 밖에 없단 말이야, 너도 알지. 난 쇼핑몰에 가서 대체품을 살 수 없다고."

빙키는 그녀에게 활짝 웃었습니다. "난 네가 아서랑 더 춤추고 싶은 것 같네."

page 56

"그렇지 않아! 자, 집중해. 다음 동작이야."

맥그래디 부인은 손뼉을 쳤습니다. "자, 모두 행진해요!"

빙키와 프랜신은 팔짱을 끼고 원 주위를 걸었습니다. 그들이 아서와 머피를 지나갈 때, 아서는 그들이 어떻게 하고 있는지 보려고 자신의 고개를 돌렸습니다.

빙키는 미소 지었습니다. "질투 나?" 그가 물었습니다.

"아서!" 머피가 말했습니다. "우리는 뒤떨어지고 있어. 집중해!"

그녀가 그를 앞으로 잡아당겼습니다.

아서는 똑바로 앞을 보았습니다. 그는 머피와 춤추고 있는 데 집중하려고 노

력했지만, 그는 프랜신에 대해 생각하고 있는 자신을 발견했습니다. 머피는 춤을 못 추는 것은 아니었지만, 그녀는 스퀘어댄스에 대한 프랜신의 열정이 없었습니다.

"머피." 아서가 속삭였습니다. "넌 네 발을 구르면서 '이-랏'하고 소리치고 싶지 않니?"

page 57

"내가 왜 그래야 해?" 머피가 속삭이며 답했습니다. "모든 춤은 따라가야 할 스텝이 있어. 난 조심하고 있다고. 난 적절한 시간에 올바른 스텝을 따라가야 해."

"이제 바늘에 실을 꿰세요!" 맥그래디 부인이 말했습니다.

아이들은 두 줄로 서기 시작하며, 손을 높이 들어 터널을 만들었습니다. 짝들이 자리를 잡으려고 서로 밀치다가, 아서는 갑자기 자신이 프랜신과 마주보며 손을 잡고 있는 것을 발견했습니다.

"너 여기서 뭐 하는 거야?" 아서가 말했습니다. "나랑 춤추려고 하는 것 좀 그만둬."

"*내가 너랑 춤추려고 하고 있다고? 나랑 춤추려고 하는 사람은 바로 너잖아!*"

"프랜신, 내가 너에게 자세히 설명해야 하니?"

"*내가 말하게 하지 마, 아서!*"

그들 두 사람 모두 깊게 숨을 들이마셨습니다.

page 59

"난 널 사랑하지 않아!" 그들은 함께 말했습니다.

10장

page 60

잠시동안 아서와 프랜신은 둘 다 깜짝 놀랐습니다. 그들은 입이 떡 벌어진 채로 서로를 마주보았습니다.

프랜신이 먼저 말을 할 수 있게 되었습니다.

"네 말은, 네가 나한테 반하지 않았다는 거야?" 그녀가 말했습니다.

아서의 입이 홱 닫혔습니다. "절대로 아니야! 난 반하지 않았어. 하지만 너는 어떤데?"

프랜신이 얼굴을 찡그렸습니다. "나도 반하지 않았어."

"하지만 너 나한테 키스하고 싶진 않아?"

"지금 농담하는 거지? 차라리 머리에 이가 생기는 편이 낫겠어."

"으으으, 역겨워." 가까이에 서 있던, 프루넬라가 말했습니다.

page 61

갑자기 아서와 프랜신은 춤이 끝났

고 모든 사람이 그들을 쳐다보고 있다는 것을 깨달았습니다. 이 상황은 당혹스러울 수 있었습니다. 사실, 당혹스러웠습니다. 하지만 갑자기 아서와 프랜신 둘 다 이 모든 것이 너무 우습다는 것을 깨달았고 웃음을 터뜨리고 말았습니다.

"하지만 나는 생각했는데—." 프랜신이 말하기 시작했습니다.

"뭐, 나는 확신했다고—." 아서가 더듬거리며 답했습니다.

"좋아요." 맥그래디 부인이 말했습니다. "구경거리는 끝났어요. 모두, 파트너를 잡으세요!"

음악이 다시 시작되었습니다. 아서는 프랜신을 향해 돌아섰습니다. 그는 작게 인사했습니다.

"제가 이 춤을 함께 춰도 되겠습니까?" 그가 물었습니다.

프랜신이 살짝 무릎을 굽히며 인사하며 답했습니다. "네, 그러죠."

"우리는 어떡하고?" 머피가 물었습니다. 빙키는 그녀 옆에 서 있었습니다.

"걱정하지 마." 프랜신이 말했습니다. "너희에겐 여전히—"

"서로가 있잖아." 아서가 그녀를 대신해서 말을 마쳤습니다.

page 63

"좋아, 빙키." 머피가 말하면서, 한숨과 함께 자신의 손을 내밀었습니다. "다시 한 번 해보자."

아서와 프랜신이 원을 그리며 깡충깡충 뛰어다니기 시작할 때, 프랜신이 활짝 웃었습니다. "휴, 난 그게 끝나서 좋아." 그녀가 말했습니다.

"나도." 아서가 말했습니다. "이제 우리 사이에 사랑처럼 바보 같은 일이 다시는 끼어들지 못하게 하자."

"네가 중요한 말을 했어, 파트너! 만약 내가 적어도 1년 동안 그 스으로 시작하는 단어를 다시 듣지 않는다 해도, 그건 여전히 너무 빠를 거야. 자, 이 나머지 애들에게 어떻게 스텝을 밟고 소란스럽게 하는지 보여주자."

그리고 두 친구는 종이 칠 때까지 열정적으로 춤을 추었습니다.

Chapter 1

1. C Outside Lakewood Elementary School, it was raining hard. But inside the gym, it was nice and dry, and the students were dancing to country music. Square dancing was a school tradition on rainy days.

2. A Arms swinging madly, Binky hoedowned backward to his spot. His elbow knocked the Brain to one side. The Brain stepped on Sue Ellen's foot. Sue Ellen slipped and fell onto Francine. In another moment, they were all slipping, falling, and most of all, complaining.

3. C Muffy folded her arms, too. "Well, if you must know, I was just saying what a crummy day this was." Arthur nodded. "I don't like the rain, either." "No, not that," said Muffy. "I'm talking about the dancing." "Oh, that," said Francine, laughing. "You did have your hands full. But I think Binky's getting better."

4. B Muffy snorted. "Maybe so, but I don't know if I'll survive another hoedown like that." She suddenly brightened. "Hey, Arthur! Next time we have square dancing, will you be my partner?"

5. B Arthur looked from one friend to the other. "Don't I get a say in this?" he asked. "No!" said Francine. "But—," Muffy started to argue. "Come on, Arthur," Francine cut in. "I'll give you a lift home."

Chapter 2

1. B Muffy sat down on a bench and sighed. The rain had stopped, and the sun was peeking out from behind the clouds, but that didn't help. Her mood was still dark.

2. B "Yes," Muffy agreed. "Some other reason—like a dancing partner who's always stepping on my toes." Binky nodded. "Not very considerate. You should tell—hey, that couldn't be it. I mean, I was your dancing partner."

3. A "But when Mrs. MacGrady says 'Swing your partner,' she doesn't mean my feet should leave the floor." "I noticed no one else was doing it my way. I just figured their partners weren't strong enough."

4. D No, no, she's a good dancer. It's just that she won't share Arthur with me. I mean, he's not her personal property. So why should she get to decide who he dances with? The way she acts, you'd think they were married or something."

5. C Suddenly his eyes grew wide. There could be one reason Francine wouldn't want to share Arthur. It would also explain why they went off arm in arm. "Wow! I guess Arthur and Francine must be in love." Binky shuddered. "I think I'm going to be sick."

Chapter 3

1. A As Arthur rode his bike to school the next morning, he was still thinking about the day before. Something was going on between Muffy and Francine— that much was certain.

2. C "Hi, Binky," said Arthur. "Good morning, Loverboy. Where's your girlfriend?"

3. B The thought of him and her, the two of them together, was ridiculous. Absurd. Silly. Goofy. In fact, when he stopped to really think about it, the idea was pretty funny.

4. D Francine reached into her locker. "Hold on, Arthur," she said. "I've got a surprise for you. Look!" She fished out two cowboy hats.

5. B "Don't ask me why. Anyway, I thought we could wear them the next time there's a square dance."

Chapter 4

1. C Later that afternoon, Francine and Muffy were changing clothes in the girls locker room. They were getting ready to play baseball.

2. A "Hey, Muffy," said Francine. "I've got a new glove to break in today. Do you want to use my old one? It's the best!"

3. C Muffy inspected it. "Too bad my hand's so small. I don't think your glove will fit properly."

4. D Arthur looked surprised. "Her special glove? The one she won the

championship with?"

5. A "Ooooooh, Arthur!" cooed Binky. His doubts had all been swept away. Francine would never have let him use her glove in a million years. But it seemed that Arthur was different. Special, even. Now Binky had all the proof he needed.

Chapter 5

1. A Arthur was sitting in a booth at the Sugar Bowl. He was drinking a milk shake and waiting for Francine to arrive.

2. B She nodded. "Arthur, you told me to meet you here and not tell anyone. You said to make sure I wasn't followed and to double back on my tracks. I feel like a spy."

3. D He pushed away his milk shake, trying to collect his thoughts. "Hey, are you going to finish that?" she asked. Arthur shook his head.

4. B "All right. Let me put it a different way. Suppose there were these two, um, dolphins. And they did a lot of stuff together. But they didn't think the same way about everything. And one day it happened that—"

5. C Arthur was still looking out the window. Now Binky and the Brain were doubled over, laughing. Suddenly Arthur stood up. "Oh, nothing! Forget I ever said anything. Bye."

Chapter 6

1. D That night Arthur called Buster on the phone. "I need some advice," he said. "Gee, Arthur, you sound so serious." "That's because I need serious advice."

2. D "Because," Buster went on, "it's really hard for me to tell if you're kidding over the phone. I mean, I can't see your face. Your face always gives you away, Arthur. But since I can't—"

3. C "It's hard to know with girls," said Buster. "They can be very mysterious. Maybe you'd better keep away from her."

4. B   Arthur slumped down in his chair. His eyes were open in shock. "Arthur!" Buster called out. "Are you okay? Arthur?" Arthur hung up the phone in a daze. He went up to his room, lay down on his bed, and stared at the ceiling.

5. A   "Mr. and Mrs. Read" said the doctor, "I'm afraid I have some bad news. Your son has cooties." "Oh, no!" cried Mrs. Read. "My baby!"

Chapter 7

1. A   Mr. Read nodded. "I used to have days like that. Especially in good weather." He glanced out the window. "But that's not a problem today. It looks like rain."

2. D   Arthur looked down at his plate. Without even thinking about it, he had rearranged his scrambled eggs into the shape of a heart.

3. B   D.W. didn't care. "My teacher says it's good to be curious about things."

4. D   "Me, too," said Arthur. Then he brushed off his shoulder where Francine had touched him. He didn't know that much about cooties, but it was better not to take any chances.

5. D   "Well, let me see . . . You're jumpy. You're nervous. Oh, and there's the fact that you're about to go into the girls' bathroom." Arthur jerked his hand back from the door. "Ah . . . I was just kidding. It was a joke."

Chapter 8

1. C   Even though Francine thought Arthur was acting strange, she still saved him a seat at lunch. "Over here, Arthur!" she called out, waving to him across the crowded cafeteria. Arthur pretended not to see her. He tried to sit at a table of fourth graders. They reluctantly made room for him.

2. B   "Did you hear something?" one of them asked. "I think it was a bug," said another. "I wish that bug would buzz off," said a third. "I don't like it being here."

3. C   Arthur looked up. Francine was standing beside him. "Why are you

sitting over here?" she asked. "I was saving you a seat. Didn't you see me waving?"

4. A Arthur smiled at the rest of the table. "She's a friend. Not a girlfriend or anything like that. Just a friend who happens to be a girl. That makes sense, doesn't it?"

5. C Prunella sighed. "It's a burden, I know. And with that burden comes responsibility." "What do you mean?" "Well, you have to tell Arthur the truth—that you don't love him. But you also have to be careful. You don't want to break his heart."

Chapter 9

1. B "Okay," said Arthur. "Maybe we shouldn't dance—" "With each other," Francine finished for him.

2. B They looked around for other partners. Arthur paired off with Muffy, while Francine stood next to Binky.

3. A Mrs. MacGrady clapped her hands. "Now, everybody promenade!" Binky and Francine walked arm-in-arm around the circle. As they passed Arthur and Muffy, Arthur turned his head to see how they were doing.

4. D Arthur looked straight ahead. He tried to concentrate on dancing with Muffy, but he found himself thinking about Francine. Muffy wasn't a bad dancer, but she didn't have Francine's enthusiasm for square dancing.

5. C "Francine, do I have to spell it out for you?" "Don't make me say it, Arthur!" They both took a deep breath. "I'M NOT IN LOVE WITH YOU!" they said together.

Chapter 10

1. B For a moment, both Arthur and Francine were stunned. They faced each other open-mouthed. Francine was the first to find her voice.

2. C "But don't you want to kiss me?" "Are you kidding? I'd rather have head lice." "Ewwww, gross," said Prunella, who was standing nearby.

3. C Suddenly Arthur and Francine realized that the dance had ended and everyone was staring at them. This could have been embarrassing. Actually, it was embarrassing. But suddenly both Arthur and Francine realized the whole thing was so ridiculous that they burst out laughing.

4. A "Whew, I'm glad that's over," she said. "Me, too," said Arthur. "Let's never let a silly thing like love come between us again."

5. D "You said a mouthful, pardner! If I don't hear the L-word again for at least a year, it will be too soon. Now, let's show the rest of these folks how to step out and raise some dust." And the two friends danced like crazy till the bell rang.

아서와 사랑에 빠진 사람은 누구?
(Who's in Love with Arthur)

1판 1쇄   2016년 1월 4일
1판 7쇄   2020년 8월 7일

지은이   Marc Brown
기획   이수영
책임편집   김보경 정소이
콘텐츠제작및감수   롱테일북스 편집부
저작권   김보경
마케팅   김보미 정경훈

펴낸이   이수영
펴낸곳   (주)롱테일북스
출판등록   제2015-000191호
주소   04043 서울특별시 마포구 양화로 12길 16-9(서교동) 북앤빌딩 3층
전자메일   helper@longtailbooks.co.kr
(학원 · 학교에서 본도서를 교재로 사용하길 원하시는 경우 전자메일로 문의주시면
자세한 안내를 받으실 수 있습니다.)

ISBN 979-11-86701-06-5 14740

롱테일북스는 (주)북하우스 퍼블리셔스의 계열사입니다.

이 도서의 국립중앙도서관 출판시도서목록(CIP)은 서지정보유통지원시스템 홈페이지(http://seoji.nl.go.kr)와
국가자료공동목록시스템(http://www.nl.go.kr/kolisnet)에서 이용하실 수 있습니다. (CIP 제어번호 : CIP 2015033030)